CULT

A Survival Guide to Customs and Etiquette

FRANCE

Sally Adamson Taylor

Marshall Cavendish
Editions

Photo Credits:
All photos by the author except pages 3, 122, 209 (Corel Stock Photo Library); 70, 128, 158, 193, (HBL Network Photo Agency) and 14, 17, 30, 52, 63, 104, 118, 144, 156, 161, 175 (David Simson). ▪ Cover photo: Masterfile/Jeremy Woodhouse.

All illustrations by TRIGG

First published in1988
Copyright © 2005 Marshall Cavendish International (Asia) Private Limited

Published by Marshall Cavendish Editions
An imprint of Marshall Cavendish International
1 New Industrial Road, Singapore 536196

Other Marshall Cavendish Offices:
Marshall Cavendish Ltd. 119 Wardour Street, London W1F OUW, UK ▪ Marshall Cavendish Corporation. 99 White Plains Road, Tarrytown NY 10591-9001, USA ▪ Marshall Cavendish Beijing. D31A, Huatingjiayuan, No. 6, Beisihuanzhonglu, Chaoyang District, Beijing, The People's Republic of China, 100029 ▪ Marshall Cavendish International (Thailand) Co Ltd. 253 Asoke, 12th Flr, Sukhumvit 21 Road, Klongtoey Nua, Wattana, Bangkok 10110, Thailand ▪ Marshall Cavendish (Malaysia) Sdn Bhd, Times Subang, Lot 46, Subang Hi-Tech Industrial Park, Batu Tiga, 40000 Shah Alam, Selangor Darul Ehsan, Malaysia

Marshall Cavendish is a trademark of Times Publishing Limited

National Library Board Singapore Cataloguing in Publication Data
Taylor, Sally Adamson.
CultureShock! : France / Sally Adamson Taylor. – Singapore : Marshall Cavendish Editions, 2005.
p. cm. – (CultureShock!)
Includes bibliographical references and index.
ISBN : 981-261-121-5
1. Etiquette – France. 2. France – Social life and customs. I. Title.
II. Series: CultureShock!
DC33.7
944 -- dc21   SLS2005032187

Printed in Singapore by Times Graphics Pte Ltd

ABOUT THE SERIES

Culture shock is a state of disorientation that can come over anyone who has been thrust into unknown surroundings, away from one's comfort zone. *CultureShock!* is a series of trusted and reputed guides which has, for decades, been helping expatriates and long-term visitors to cushion the impact of culture shock whenever they move to a new country.

Written by people who have lived in the country and experienced culture shock themselves, the authors share all the information necessary for anyone to cope with these feelings of disorientation more effectively. The guides are written in a style that is easy to read and covers a range of topics that will arm readers with enough advice, hints and tips to make their lives as normal as possible again.

Each book is structured in the same manner. It begins with the first impressions that visitors will have of that city or country. To understand a culture, one must first understand the people—where they came from, who they are, the values and traditions they live by, as well as their customs and etiquette. This is covered in the first half of the book

Then on with the practical aspects—how to settle in with the greatest of ease. Authors walk readers through how to find accommodation, get the utilities and telecommunications up and running, enrol the children in school and keep in the pink of health. But that's not all. Once the essentials are out of the way, venture out and try the food, enjoy more of the culture and travel to other areas. Then be immersed in the language of the country before discovering more about the business side of things.

To round off, snippets of basic information are offered before readers are 'tested' on customs and etiquette of the country. Useful words and phrases, a comprehensive resource guide and list of books for further research are also included for easy reference.

CONTENTS

FOREWORD

Like many of my generation, I started travelling abroad the summer after my university studies were complete. When I first set my naive American Anglo-Saxon foot on a Paris sidewalk in 1970, I was so intimidated by the French hauteur that I determined to have nothing more to do with that country or those people. Today, I am a devoted Francophile. Though I still find Parisians a little difficult at times, I am very grateful for the time I can spend among them.

Between hate and love, the French say, there is just one step. For me, it was several steps. I credit the many wines of France and the peaceful back roads that meander through her vineyards for my first seduction. I discovered many patient and generous French people who actually welcomed a single lady cyclist arriving at their winery and tolerated her horrible high school French. The dark shades of doubt dropped and I began to see the bright wonders of these people, their countryside, and, of course, their most remarkable gift to the world, Paris.

ACKNOWLEDGEMENTS

In trying to shorten the steps for the readers, I have tempered my own views with the observations and wisdom of a great many others. Of the many who have made personal and intellectual contributions to this project, I would like to particularly thank Sam Abt, my first French teacher Mme Albaugh (wherever she is), Elizabeth Antebi, Adeline & Renaud de Barry, Barbara Bell, Fiona Beeston, Paul Bertier, Isabelle Bolgert, Rebecca Boone, Michele Brothers, Chuck Canapa, Raymonde Carroll, Mouloud Chekini, John & Nona Denis, Patricia Dunn, Lena Emmery, Nathalie Fieldel-Schact, Therese de Gasquet, Mary de Vachon, Franck Gauthey, Ruth & Lew Goldhammer, Kim Guptill, Gus Hawkins, Neil Hollander, Francis Kelsall, Christy Love, Lucien Legrand, Régine Michel, Robert Moran, Ivy & Chandran Nair, Radha Nair, Polly Platt, Rod Shippey, Janine & Charles Stockton, my mother Ann Adamson Taylor (a pioneer in intercultural relationships), Susan Troccolo, Shuji Yoshida, Rob & Neil van der Plas, Susan Wagner, Esther Wanning, and the women at WICE, AAWE and Bloom.

San Francisco, 2005

Thanks, also, to fellow Francophile, Christopher Pitts, who did all the research for the updates in the 2003 edition of *CultureShock! France*.

MAP OF FRANCE

ENGLAND

NETHERLANDS

BELGIUM

GERMANY

ENGLISH CHANNEL

←LUXEMBOURG

● PARIS

SWITZERLAND

ATLANTIC
OCEAN

FRANCE

BAY OF
BISCAY

ITALY

CORSE

SPAIN

ANDORRA

MEDITERRANEAN SEA

FIRST IMPRESSIONS

'... we are caught between the desire to deny differences (we are all human) and the desire to emphasise them (the right to be different).'
—Raymonde Carroll, *Cultural Misunderstandings*

LEARNING TO UNDERSTAND
(AND LOVE) THE FRENCH

Culture shock can be reduced considerably if you know something about how the French see themselves, both in public life and in private life. Among the many helpful sources for this book, the insights of Raymonde Carroll in *Cultural Misunderstandings* ('*Evidence Invisible*' in French) have been my biggest inspiration. A French woman trained as an anthropologist and married to an American, Dr Carroll has developed an excellent approach to avoiding false assumptions when studying cultural attitudes.

Cultural analysis is an act of humility, says Dr Carroll, in which you attempt to forget, for a moment, your own way of seeing and briefly replace it with another way, knowing you can never adopt that other way, only assert its validity. One can live a long time in another culture and never understand it. It is too easy to treat opaque situations as if they were transparent, and thus never really understand them. Like the process of learning another language, cultural understanding is difficult and sometimes painfully slow. But the more you learn, the more perceptive you become.

As Raymonde Carroll explains, '… one of the great advantages of cultural analysis, aside from that of expanding our horizons,

'Ce qu'il y a de plus étranger en France, pour les Français, c'est la France.' (What is most foreign in France, for the French, is France.)
—Modeste Mignon Balzac

In Paris, life is on the street, but privacy is sacred.

is that of transforming our cultural misunderstandings from a source of occasionally deep wounds into a fascinating and inexhaustible exploration of the other.'

We hope this book will begin your love affair with the French.

BEING SOMEONE

People vary enormously in their ability to adapt to new environments. Your success in France will depend, fundamentally, on your tolerance for ambiguity. A new cultural environment guarantees opaque situations, times when you think you are doing everything correctly and nothing is working. If you have had previous experiences living successfully outside of your birth culture, then you are well on your way. If this is your first time in a foreign culture with a foreign language, just keep reading.

Learning the second culture, like learning the second language, is usually the hardest. It is humbling. You realise that the way you think and behave is not something unique in our personality, or generally accepted as polite or reasonable among fellow humans. It is just something your own momma taught you.

The Rooster

Too often one hears people say that they love France, but hate the French. To them, we offer the retort of American Parisian and Francophile, Gertrude Stein, "How can foreigners say they like France but not the French? It's the French who made the France they like—and it is the French who keep it that way."

Everyone with a Western education knows something of the art, history and politics of this country. It should come as no surprise that the French are proud of their remarkable heritage. And they are not ashamed to 'crow' about it.

The French even use the rooster as their national symbol. (This is a very old play on words. Two thousand years ago, the Latin word for France was Gaul, which also means 'rooster' in Latin.) Not only does the rooster crow loudly, he struts about, holding himself aloof from the other animals in the barnyard. He considers himself superior to all who neglect to challenge his authority. He is a bit laughable, but he gets away with it by posturing.

The French readily admit their tendencies towards posturing and self-promotion. They can't explain it, either. But you can't help admiring the way they have successfully promoted their wines, perfumes, fashion houses and aeronautics, even their country, to the world. They are the fourth largest economy on the planet. They know how to produce quality products and they know how to market them.

They also know how to live. This book is a toast to the French!

What makes one way of doing things 'correct' and another quite similar way 'incorrect' changes with where you are. The French have just as good reasons for doing it their way as your momma had for doing her (and in turn, your way).

We usually take our way for granted so much we can't even describe why we behave the way we do. But when you enter another culture, wow. The rules change.

Most of us learn these new rules by observation. Table manners, for example. The tools we use, how we use them, what we do with our arms, elbows, hands and mouths, all essentials of 'good table manners' will take some re-examination in France.

The French eat salad with their fork in their left hand, but pasta with their fork in their right hand. If you use a fork differently, that just marks you as a foreigner with poor table manners. If your voice can be heard by diners at other tables in a small restaurant, you will be even more harshly judged. You are now a thoughtless bore who is ruining everyone else's dining experience.

'How many cares one loses when one decides not to be something, but to be someone.'
—Gabrielle 'Coco' Chanel

In New York, everyone is boisterous in a restaurant, so the noise level makes it difficult enough just to hear the people at your own table. In France, privacy in public spaces is sacred, both yours and that of the other diners around you.

Adapting to a new culture, like learning a new language, takes observation, sensitivity, imagination and practice. You also need to be patient, with yourself and everyone else. They really do have good reasons for their peculiar tendencies. And it is not about you. Keep your sense of humour. Laugh at your ignorance or your little failures and try again.

Stretching outside your own culture enriches your perspectives on the world. As with physical fitness, the more you practise reaching out, the better you become. And the more you can enjoy the French and their wonderful country. This book is full of 'stretching' exercises. Here is just one to start.

GIVING AND GETTING DIRECTIONS— THE FIRST DANCE

One of the first things a visitor needs in a new place is directions. Most travellers carry a map and if you don't speak any French, you best carry one too. If you do speak some French, you will find the French endlessly willing to help you out. The French love to give and get directions. It is one of the few appropriate ways they can break the privacy boundary among strangers on the street.

When a French person gets lost (and many do, especially in Paris), he or she will be likely to stop YOU and ask for directions. It will be done with courtesy, even hesitancy and with apologies for disturbing you. (Polly Platt in her book *French or Foe?* calls these her ten magic words: *Excusez-moi, Monsieur, de vous déranger, mais j'ai une problème…*).

- If you are learning French, all the better. Here is your first chance to use your new skills! Since you just arrived, it is unlikely you have an answer in your first encounter. But it won't be long before you are giving and getting directions with the best of them.
- You don't speak any French? Don't panic. It is still a great compliment you have been paid. You look so at home in the neighbourhood, and you present yourself so well, you have been mistaken for a fellow French person, a trustworthy one at that. He has overcome his Gallic reserve to ask for your help. Apologise immediately, (*Desolé,*

Monsieur, je ne parle pas français) and stay to help him track down another person with the information he needs. If you are very lucky, he might switch to English. Bravo! You have a second chance to help him out.

- Only if you don't have a clue where he wants to go might you offer to pull out your map. Use a low, conspiratorial voice and say, "*J'ai un plan*". Don't actually pull it out, unless he then expresses clear interest in looking at it. Usually a map will be rejected immediately. Nobody wants to look like a tourist in their own town.

Other Books on the French

Although no book this short can provide complete cultural understanding, we can walk you through some of the early transitions necessary to really enjoy France and the French. Since the first edition of this book appeared in 1990, when it stood nearly alone, the subject of cultural understanding has blossomed into a serious social science and the peculiarities of the French taken beyond ridicule by many other authors. There are dozens of books now on the etiquette and expectations of the French, and why they are the way they are. (One of my early favourites wasn't even a guidebook: *A Year in Provence* by Peter Mayle. The best one recently is *Sixty Million Frenchmen Can't Be Wrong*.) We include a bibliography at the back of this book and credit many authors in our text. They have greatly added to our own insights.

Now, we have already stumbled upon several seeming inconsistencies in the French. A French person, a sophisticated *Parisien* no less, is willing to stop and speak with a total stranger on the street about his or her ignorance concerning which way to go, when he or she wouldn't dream of making small talk when waiting in line at the post office. This person really wants to know the way, yet clearly doesn't want to look at a map.

What is going on here? Well, finding specific destinations in Paris can be difficult. And the French have as good a sense of expediency as anybody. They also love to discuss things (as we will see later). So it seems sensible to find a person who looks like they are local and discrete and ask them. Getting out a map involves a great deal more effort, not to mention advertising to everyone on the street their embarrassing predicament. Remember that rooster! The French like to look like they are in control, even when they are not.

Getting back to the job at hand... if you speak a little French, you now have a chance to participate in your first verbal waltz. You allow the person first to apologise and complete his or her question. He or she will then wait patiently for your answer. If you don't know exactly where he or she is trying to go, send him off in the right direction, suggesting he or she ask someone at the next intersection.

The First Steps

There are certain basics of cultural survival in any country: eating, dressing and communicating. In France, each of these is an art form—which is one reason why Paris is the most popular tourist destination on earth.

- **Eating**

  The endless joy of the French is their food. Menus are studied in detail. Waiters are proud of the dishes they present and will advise you on choices as conscientiously as a doctor gives his prognosis. Two hours are often dedicated to the pleasures of lunch. The only thing you can do really wrong with eating in France is to rush it. This includes snacking in public. Sit down and join the French for a proper meal.

- **Dressing**

  The dress code in France appears to be typically Western and, especially among the young, 'anything goes'. But you will also find, especially when in Paris, that the French care a great deal about the way they dress. The streets are full of people for whom being sophisticated includes looking 'comfortable in their skin'. Enjoy the art, the architecture, the food and your

If you know where he or she is going and you have a few moments, escort him or her to the place where he wants to go. This is not required, but it is a gracious extension of the favour.

In turn, if you ask directions of a French person, you do the same. First, you apologise for disturbing him or her. (*Excusez-moi, Monsieur, de vous déranger, mais j'ai une problème…*) Then ask your question, giving him or her the courtesy of time to think and listening to the whole answer, however long it takes. Give your thanks and head off in the direction he or she has advised, even if you suspect that his or her answer is wrong.

own participation in this remarkable city in clothes that make you look your best. If you feel good about yourself and how you look, the French don't care what you wear. At the opera you'll find everything from full length gowns with diamond tiara to blue jeans and T-shirts. It's your own best taste.

- **Communicating**
  To be able to speak some French, enough to communicate basic needs and desires, will make a tremendous difference in your life in France. Most French people are very tolerant of poor French. (I know, because mine is lousy.) Once you've tried to reach out in French, they will usually reach out, too, relieved that your French is even worse than their English. We will throw in French words here and there, to help get you started, and in *Chapter 8:Learning French*, you will be provided more tips, as well as a good discussion of the many non-verbal ways the French express themselves. Persevere! You'll be challenged and rewarded time and again when you are in any Francophone country.

Why the French Hate Maps

'A map without a compass is a useless thing.'
—Charles Stockton

If you don't speak French and don't want to ask directions, you are going to have to rely on a map and a compass. It is often overcast in France and the compass will help you establish north. With any luck, someone will stop as you look at your map and offer to help you. Looking at a map in Paris is a clear signal someone is lost and foreign. (We already know the French don't look at maps.)

I love maps and the French produce fabulous ones. When I first lived in Paris and was asked directions, I would proudly reach for my lovely Paris map, only to find my interlocutor's face suddenly drop in anguish. If I actually opened the thing, he would recoil, looking desperately around for another stranger to pull into our discussion. He didn't want a map. He just wanted an answer.

The French tend to prefer asking a person for information in all things. They don't like referring to maps, guidebooks, train tables, even menus in restaurants. They want to have a dialogue with a person.

There is a good reason for this, according to Raymonde Carroll. A map gives a great deal of information that is superfluous to the problem at hand. A person, however, is likely to give only the information needed to solve the specific problem.

As you might expect, the information area *(renseignements)* at train stations in France are quite large and usually jammed with people who have taken a number and are waiting patiently for their turn to speak to someone. The answer to their question is probably found on a time table among the *horaires* (display-racks) nearby.

Such faith in human beings and unwillingness to cope with large amounts of extraneous information has created a breed of official French information-givers that can frustrate map lovers like myself. I often feel that people in France are not giving me all the information I should have. This is probably my fault. I haven't explained myself well enough in French, or I haven't engaged the fellow in polite enough conversation that he wants to volunteer extra information. He is trying to efficiently answer my question. We will talk more about the art of getting information in France in a later chapter.

What? French people will give a wrong answer? Only if they don't know the right one. They are not trying to trick you, but they would rather offer a guess than nothing at all. That would be both shirking their duty to you and failing to look intelligent. So pick your person carefully (not too roostery) and feel free to ask him or her first if he or she lives in the *quartier* (the neighbourhood).

Here is how one French friend of mine picks someone to ask directions: "I ask a man or woman who looks intelligent. Not anyone old and slow, who probably doesn't leave the area very often and won't be able to organise his thoughts quickly. I look for efficient-looking people, serious people carrying an attaché case, for example, and walking confidently. I don't ask young people; they might be too shy or too fresh." (You see now how flattered you can feel for being asked yourself?)

Usually, your new French confidant will then escort you to your destination. If he or she leaves you to it, and you don't at least start out in the direction he or she indicated, and continue until he or she is out of sight, he or she may well race after you to correct your error. (This is another remarkable trait of the French we will explore later in the book. They take to heart any responsibility for you that they have accepted.)

FROM THE CELTS TO ROLLERBLADES

CHAPTER 2

'In France... it is impossible to disassociate the past
from the present. There is no clear line to divide
ancient from modern France, and what goes
for architecture goes for the people, too'
—Jean-Benoît Nadeau and Julie Barrow,
Sixty Million Frenchmen Can't Be Wrong

THE CIRCLES OF FRENCH LIFE

In 1787, English statesman Horace Walpole complained of the French 'insistent airs of superiority'. Back then, they had a right to them. For 200 years, all civilised people in the Western world spoke and read French. International business and diplomacy were conducted nearly exclusively in French up until World War I.

Today, the French have graciously learned some English, and even some Japanese, yet they do retain a great sense of dignity about their country, a love of their language and a *joie de vivre*, an enjoyment of life—making France special.

Dress and architecture in France say a great deal about how the French relate to each other and to the world. And where they get that sense of superiority. One of the first things you will notice across France is the unique radiating star patterns of the roads and streets.

The whole country is organised in these wheels, or circles. And all roads eventually lead to Paris. To some extent, the French operate in circles. Interlocking circles of relationship link the private worlds of family, sex and friends, with the public worlds of art, work, architecture and politics. There is a *grand philosophie* for living among the French and these circles help remind us of that.

The supreme example in Paris street planning is the circle around the Arc de Triomphe, affectionately known as the Etoile, the Star. A dozen grand boulevards lead to this Star.

Even the pedestrian crossing around the Etoile are tricky.

Each offers a dramatic angle of the mighty Arch, usually flying a huge tricolor French flag, the country's national symbol since 1790.

You can see straight down the Champs Elysée east to the Concorde and the Louvre and west all the way out to La Defense and the new Arch. Talk about city planning! Here are hundreds of years of rights-of-way (originating with the layout of the royal hunting grounds) still working and still developing.

Once you reach the Arch, however, you face half a dozen lanes of traffic going around it, each vehicle seeking its preference among 12 exits, with no visible evidence of established rules or priorities.

In the following chapters, we will describe how to manage yourself inside and through the many circles of French life, how you need to look and act, both to enjoy yourself and to accomplish your objectives. Perhaps even to survive!

Living in a Circular System

Edward T. Hall in his book *The Hidden Dimension* talks about the sociopetal or socially-centred aspects of the French. They connect all points and all functions to centre points, in geography, in society and in business.

"It is incredible how many facets of French life the radiating star pattern touches," Hall says. "It is almost as though the whole culture were set up on a model in which power, influence and control flowed in and out from a series of interlocking centres."

This sort of organisation demands you start out in the right direction in the first place, otherwise you get progressively off base. The wrong turn off the Etoile, for example, will lead you further and further from your goal. In a square grid pattern, like the ancient planned city of Xian, China, or New York City today, you have many ways to reach a destination, all equally workable.

Living in this circular system, a French person will consider all his options, first. He will establish his goal and the best plan for getting there, before he takes his first step. A Chinese or an American, on the other hand, will charge right out in the general direction, figuring he can amend his way as he goes along. This emphasis on goals among the Gauls pervades many aspects of French life, including language and politics.

THE EARLY FRENCH

Evidence of human communities date back 30,000 years in this part of Europe. In Brittany, the western extreme of the country, stone monoliths at Carnac, 4,000 years old, are credited to the Beaker people. While little is known of these people, they lurk in the genes of the French. In *Sixty Million Frenchmen Can't Be Wrong,* the Canadian authors report: "It occurred to us that the French are really the Aborigines of France. The word *aborigines* is usually associated with primitive peoples now, but it really just means 'original'. The ancestors of the French go back several ice ages. They are not a people who, like North Americans, arrived in the midst of a primitive

The French

'France is a hodgepodge. There were the Gauls (though nobody knows what they were), who adopted the Roman culture and language quite willingly. Saxon, Viking, Moorish, and English invaders came and went after that. Only centuries later did national identities start to emerge in Europe. The people you meet in France are really descendants of all the tribes and races that ever invaded France, and all the immigrants that ever flocked there from other countries.'

—*Sixty Million Frenchmen Can't Be Wrong*, Jean-Benoît Nadeau & Julie Barlow culture, erased it, and started over. They have always been there."

In 900 BC, Celtic tribes began spreading west across the Rhine and by the 5th century BC, they dominated most of France and Belgium, with the more adventurous crossing the Atlantic to the British Isles.

The Celts were not an homogenous people, but organised into small, fierce tribes, speaking different languages and constantly fighting among themselves. They adjusted to the geography where they settled. We know so little of the people who were already there, we must assume they were assimilated.

In the mountains of what we now call Switzerland, the Helvetii established dominance. In the north-west, the Belgae fended off the Scandinavian tribes. The Celtic people in the south dwelt among the Greeks (Phoenicians), who are credited with founding the city of Massilia (now Marseille in French, Marseilles in English) in 600 BC.

The Romans called the land of these Celtic peoples Gaul or Gallia. In 121 BC, they conquered the Mediterranean coastline, and most of what is now the Provence and Languedoc. Julius Caesar then won domination over the rest of what was to become France during the Gallic Wars, 58–51 BC. (The feistier Celtic tribes in Brittany successfully resisted. So did the Celts who had settled in Cornwall, Wales and Scotland.)

The Romans built major edifices you can still visit today, and the people were somewhat assimilated into the Empire. Emperor Claudius I, a Roman born in the city that is now Lyon (Lyons in English) even admitted Gallic noblemen to the Roman Senate. The exports of wine, food and pottery prospered, as it still does today.

The Romans brought their language, law and Christianity, but the Celtic tribes retained many of their unique ways, still evident in the various regions of the country today. Eventually, the Roman Empire weakened and various Germanic tribes invaded. The Visigoths took the south, Acquitaine and the Provence; the Franks won Paris and northern Gaul; and the Alamani and Burgundians dominated to the east as far west as the Soane River Valley.

Statue of Charlemagne outside Notre Damelle.

Clovis, King of the Franks, and a Christian, rousted the last Romans in AD 486 and unified the country, giving it the Germanic name. But the country remained a collection of distinct tribes and languages.

In AD 800, Charlemagne was crowned Holy Roman Emperor, and though the realm disintegrated after his death, France remained thereafter a blending of Celtic, Roman and Frankish peoples. For the many wonderful books on the history of France, please refer to the *Further Reading* section at the back of this book. Meanwhile, suffice it to say that for another 700 years, squabbling among themselves and with the British, the French were defined as much by geography and their local leaders as by the Church and the King.

The 16th century brought the discovery of the New World, the rediscovery and proliferation of the sciences, and Gutenberg's printing press to spread the news. With this explosion in intellectual energy, King of Francois the First gathered Europe's artists and scientists to his capitol, Paris, making France a centre of the Renaissance.

Louis XIV reigned for over 70 years, during which time France became the model of culture in Europe. While England was in civil war, French expeditions spread out across the high seas, gaining great wealth and civilising, they thought, the world.

By the time of the French Revolution, at the end of the 18th century, France led the world, in the arts and in philosophy. Her people had a strong desire for self-determination, but no clue yet as to how to govern themselves. Half of the population still didn't speak French, though the Académie Française, to protect and promote French, had been established in 1635.

By 1790, they had their tricolor flag, but it would be another century before France had a functional democracy. Napoleon came to power in 1799 with monarchy as his model. His nephew, Louis Napoleon Bonaparte, made a bigger stretch, declaring himself the second Augustus Caesar. He set his sights on making Paris the new Rome.

Thanks to his architect, Baron Georges Haussmann, Paris became in just 20 years the 'City of Light' and the architectural envy of the world. Her many urban centres, each a gem of one period or another, are showcased by streets connected in star patterns, grand boulevards lined with elegant architecture, crossing at odd angles. It makes driving through Paris a nightmare and walking through Paris joy.

SOME RECENT HISTORY

Charles de Gaulle, leader of the French Resistance during World War II and beloved president of France in the 1960s, revived the old perception that France leads the world down the path of civilisation. "La France est la lumière du monde, son génie est d'illuminer l'Univers (France is the light of the world, her genius lights the universe)," he said.

Even in 1981, when François Mitterrand accepted the job of President, he said, "A just and generous France... can light the path of mankind." The French still love to hear it and many of us Francophiles believe it. France welcomes more visitors each year than her total population. In spite of a century that has not been kind to France, Paris remains the most architecturally beautiful city in the world, and the French believe in their mission to civilise the rest of us.

(No need to remind the French that the main reason they still have their beautiful Paris, castles, cathedrals and cities is because they were forced to surrender to the Nazis.)

World War I destroyed nearly two million of the brightest and best of the French male population, and the years leading up to World War II did not revive the French economy or her spirit. France had the oldest population in Europe. She lost 130,000 men in six weeks fighting against the technologically superior Germans before surrendering 22 June 1940. While many French fought in the Resistance, World War II still lives in the memories of many French people as a time of disgrace under German domination.

The Allied victory brought France her freedom, but she was economically and politically destitute. War hero Charles de Gaulle became the Premier of a provisional government. Then in 1946, the Fourth Republic was formed (fourth, that is, since the Revolution), but the political structure proved unstable time and again. There were 22 governments in 12 years.

Finally, in 1958, de Gaulle led a coup, establishing the Fifth Republic, which gave greater constitutional powers to the president and political stability. In spite of a bitter war in Algeria, he remained popular at home. The economy revived, thanks in part to a more stable political structure and a well educated cadre of administrators.

France still functions under this Fifth Republic. The French still relish some echoes of monarchy. The president lives in the 18th century Elysée palace, home of Madame de Pompadour, two Napoleons, and the official residence of the presidents of France since 1873. A quiet and relatively impoverished titled class still pass along their titles and enjoy status. Most important, there are 500 *grande écoles* in France which train most of the country's elite. These are not universities, but very competitive training schools from which nearly all leaders of commerce and of the country are selected, based on their grades at these schools.

The presidency passed from de Gaulle to Georges Pompidou to Valérie Giscard d'Estaing, a graduate of the top École Nationale d'Administration (ENA). All these first presidents were members of the conservative Rally for the Republic party (RPR) .

François Mitterrand, a Socialist, won the election in 1981 by just 51 per cent as the right split its votes between the parties of Giscard and Jacques Chirac. (On his third try 14 years later, Chirac finally became the President, and retained his position as Mayor of France along with it.)

Mitterrand's victory was the first time since 1936 that a coalition of centrists, socialists and communists had won a presidential election. Everybody expected big changes in government policy. Some changes came, but few were effective. Meanwhile, conservative capitalists' money poured out of France.

Mitterrand fulfilled his election promises: five weeks of paid vacation, a 10 per cent increase in salaries and optional retirement at 60. He nationalised much of the public service sector, including many banks, fuel and power suppliers, steel factories, and some electronics, chemical and telecommunication firms. (Many aspects of French industry, particularly banking, had been in the hands of the government since World War II, in spite of capitalist leadership.)

The new Auroux laws strengthened the powers of the unions in the nationalised companies. At the time, approximately 30 per cent of the workforce were in government jobs. Today, it is closer to 40 per cent, but none of Mitterrand's moves changed the basic centralised power structure of France.

By 1985, with the European economy in crisis and the French franc falling, voters began to lose faith in the Socialists. In 1986, the RPR returned to power in the Assembly and Mitterrand was forced to 'cohabit' as President with RPR's Jacques Chirac as prime minister. Chirac (also an ENA grad, or *énarque*) was already the first Mayor of Paris (The first because Paris had before been run before by the 20 *arrondissement* mayors).

A pupil of Georges Pompidou, Chirac privatised a number of state-run organisations and the forces of the socialist movement seemed doomed. Mitterrand rallied in 1988, regaining the Assembly and chose Michel Rocard (another socialist, but also an *énarque*) as his prime minister. Chirac returned in 1995, winning the presidency. He made a 35-hour work week compulsory, hoping to reduce unemployment. That law has just recently (2005) been watered down, as angry protestors reminded the Government it had failed to accomplish its goal.

Chirac was re-elected in 2002 with 82 per cent of the vote. His current prime minister is Jean Pierre Raffarin. Both men are of the new Union for the Presidential Majority party (UMP) and remain in power until the next national elections in 2007. For a fascinating discussion of the way the French political system works, don't miss *Sixty Million Frenchmen Can't Be Wrong*.

How They Vote

The legal voting age is 18 in France, and elections are always held on Sundays, with local candidates required to gain 50 per cent of the voting total. With several different party 'lists', often a run-off election must be held the subsequent Sunday to get a majority decision. In the second try, various parties will pool their votes to give one candidate a majority, so loyalties must be flexible as compromise is inevitable.

The biggest ongoing issue of the 1990s for France was the European Union. While the concept of a united Europe was born in France (always bringing those marbles together in a jar), the concept found little nourishment from French farmers and factory workers. Hurt by new GATT trade agreements, the French workers faced a world economic recession and an increasing number of foreign-born Frenchmen taking their jobs. The Maastricht Treaty only passed in France by 51 per cent.

On 1 January 1999, the dear old French franc passed into oblivion. The euro was launched as the currency of Europe more swiftly and successfully than Julius Caeser divided Gaul into three parts or TV lobotomised the planet. Fortunately, the French remain very much individuals and the wonderful marbles in their jar remain in tact, as we will see in the following chapter.

Always Expect a Gréve (Strike)

Taking to the streets in organised demonstrations is the national exercise of France. The French love to express their political opinions, individually and in groups. And their countrymen have supernatural patience with the resulting inconveniences.

Happily (for them) Paris is the transportation centre of the country, so a strike in Paris carries a powerful effect.

You might get a transportation union strike suddenly stopping all public transport in Paris, or farmers blocking the national highway system with their tractors protesting GATT accords, or parents clogging the streets lobbying for better education for their children. Any of these may come swiftly, with only a warning that morning on the radio.

Also watch out for the monthly 'Critical Mass' tour of Paris by thousands of skate boarders (*rolleurs*). Complete with police escort, they create a long river of moving bodies, blocking the major boulevards along their route. Cars and pedestrians are further policed by fellow skateboarders with badges, who won't even let a bicyclist pass through.

Taxes and Other Inconsistencies

To maintain their exquisite capital city, and the best health care system in the world, the French people are burdened by the highest level of taxation in Europe (43.8 per cent of GDP in 2003). France enjoys a mix of the traditional, the exotic, and the latest technological advances. The country is well served by their TGV trains, the fastest in the world, as

The *tabac* is ubiquitous in France for everything from political press to phone cards for your cell phone.

well as the new Eurostar, with a 3.5-hour train service, from Paris to London.

France was the third country in the world to develop a nuclear bomb and draws 65 per cent of her energy needs from nuclear power plants scattered incongruously around the beautiful countryside. Yet Parisians still prefer to buy their bread, meat and vegetables daily, fresh-from-the-farm at outdoor markets, if possible. They will walk or bicycle rather than drive. They get dressed up to run an errand to the post office.

A constant theme in conversation is the deterioration of the quality of life, while everywhere this visitor looks, its richness and diversity seems secure.

Politics is King

Four centuries of great literature and philosophy give the French a profound love of politics. While the notion of democracy was not invented in France, its principles have been fiercely defended here. To this day, the French argue continually and passionately about how these principles should be put into action.

The range of French political philosophies covers a wide spectrum, helped along by a love of analytical thinking that is the bedrock of the education system, and a free and inquiring press. (Mussolini and Hitler agreed once that France was ruined by alcohol, syphilis and journalism.)

There is nothing that the French love to read about and talk about so much as politics and philosophy. France's heroes are its 'political and literary figures' not its rock stars. You can watch 'talking heads' on TV discussing the minutiae of a political issue for hours. "How bored we would be," Chateaubriand is credited with saying, "if it were not for politics."

The minute you move among the French, you are engaged in political discussion. Your cab driver will rail against the current government, the gentleman at the next table at a café will blame the communists, and the student in your train compartment will condemn the bourgeois establishment. Everyone will want you to have an opinion, too. And they will be disappointed if you just agree with theirs.

Whether or not you speak French, you will be diving right into politics, yours, France's and everyone else's. It will help you to know something about recent political history.

STEREOTYPES AND BEYOND— THE PUBLIC FRENCH

CHAPTER 3

'An Englishman apologises when you step on his foot.
A Frenchman berates you when he steps on yours.'
—Mort Rosenblum, *Mission to Civilize*

SKIN DEEP

All of us who travel and make friends in other nations quickly learn the pitfalls of cultural stereotypes. They can easily be a barrier to cultural and human understanding. We have to look at them, but we have to get beyond them.

It is easy but pointless to rage against the 'illogical' differences between your logic and someone else's. Conversely, who wants to be pigeon-holed as someone just 'typical' of his own culture? Each of us takes pride in his own individuality, even while we make cultural assumptions of others that blind us. We are programmed by our social experience. Learning a new culture demands a reprogramming.

Cultural stereotypes have some elements of truth, valid reasons why they were formed. So let's examine some of the stereotypes now, both those you may have about the French and those the French may assume about you.

If culture is an onion, we are starting with that dry brown paper skin. No need to be thin-skinned about any of this. We all have superficial cultural biases to discard.

STEREOTYPES ABOUT THE FRENCH

The Gallic temperament has been stereotyped as cold, imperious and negative. The French even joke about it. *Le pire est toujours certain*, they say. (The worst is always certain).

To a bubbly, enthusiastic American or a polite and hesitant Asian, the typical French public behaviour seems a personal rebuff. But this behaviour has nothing to do with you. The French try hard to be cool in public, even among the French. In fact, they are full of passion.

A passionate outburst is almost guaranteed in traffic congestion or in a parking dispute. This has created another stereotype: that they are argumentative and confrontational. Yes, but they will almost never come to serious physical violence—remember that rooster in Chapter One!

In public, the French will strive to maintain their composure. They will prefer you do the same. It may appear at first that they are trying to throw you off balance with their unsmiling reserve. But don't worry, the French do not hate foreigners. In fact, they often prefer people of other nations to their own countrymen.

BEYOND THE GAULS & FRANKS

Thankfully, most of the French are conservative stay-at-homes, so strong regional differences remain in the country and the cuisine. While many of these descendants of the tribes of the Celts and the Franks have flocked to Paris and other urban centres, they visit home often. They even vote in the towns where they were born. (*We offer a brief gastronomic tour of the delicious reasons why in 'Cuisine and Character by Pays'*, Chapter 7:The Greatest Arts of France, *on page 142*).

The more recent racial and cultural additions to the make-up of the France population are more complicated. The Celts were adventurers far back in pre-history. The the Christian Crusades in the Middle Ages added a 'civilising' ideal to their travels, which continues today. It is examined in detail in a book, *Mission to Civilize* by Mort Rosenblum. (*See* Further Reading *on page 244*.)

Some of her colonies remain part of France. These Départements d'outre Mer (DOM) and Territoires d'outre Mer (TOM) are in every respect France, and their people French. While the French pride themselves on their racial and religious tolerance, they have made mistakes, like the rest of the Europeans, in dealing with former colonies, particularly Algeria.

According to Canadians Jean-Benoît Nadeau and Julie Barlow in their wonderful book *Sixty Million Frenchmen Can't Be Wrong*, the French were wrong in Algeria. Four generations of French lived and prospered in Algeria without giving the rights of citizenship to the indigenous Muslims. A brutal decade of guerilla war in Algeria and France finally ended with the return of that country to those Muslims in 1962. But the influx of Muslims into France following the war was enormous, and their assimilation into French culture was not expected.

Today, in true democratic spirit, France has extended to all her colonial conquests the privileges of being free and equal Frenchmen. (French women joined the party with full and equal rights just after World War II.) Assimilation is assumed.

Thanks to a strong central government, every French citizen in the world receives the same education, using the same curricula, and he or she is entitled to all the government services, whether in France proper or abroad in the DOMs and TOMs. Everyone is represented in the French legislature in Paris. There are even two representatives of French citizens living in the USA.

Violence, with Umbrella

The most physical violence I have seen in Paris involved a very small, elderly and refined French lady leaving the Métro. She was walking up the crowded stairs with the rest of us when suddenly, she started beating a young man with her umbrella while she screamed ferociously at him, accusing him of grabbing at her purse. The fellow backed against the wall, bowing to deflect the blows. As soon as everyone understood the purse was still safely under the lady's arm, they calmly continued their climb. I was impressed. She got everybody's attention and respect at the same time. And we had no doubts about who was in charge.

The Other French

Many people from the old colonies and from the DOMs and TOMs choose to live in France. You will find French speaking people from the Caribbean, Africa, the Middle East, Asia and the Pacific all over the country, though they tend to congregate in certain areas around Paris.

But until 1962, the major foreign presence in France was the Italians, followed by the Spaniards. The Poles, Russians, Armenians, Hungarians and Portuguese have also come to France in large numbers (over 250,000 each) during various political upheavals in their own countries in the last century. These have successfully assimilated into French culture, though you can still find some good restaurants, should you tire of French cuisine.

People of some former colonies of France, particularly the dark-skinned peoples of West Africa, the West Indies and the South Pacific, generally fare better in France than in other predominantly white countries. These French-speaking 'southerners' are generally easy-going and add variety to the mix of food and fashion. They are accepted as authentic and at the same time, French.

French Asians from Vietnam, Cambodia and China are considered honest, hard-working and colourful. They have made fine contributions to the cosmopolitan cuisine of Paris as well. You will also find many racially 'mixed' couples in France. Children of all racial and economic backgrounds enjoy the public parks in general harmony. The one group with the most difficulties assimilating are also the largest.

The Problematic Beurs

With the independence of the French colony of Algeria in 1962 came a huge influx of pro-France Muslims. The French referred to them as Arabs, and the connotation is not particularly positive. The children of these former Algerians, those born in France, are called Beurs, after the Arabic term. They make up the largest ethnic minority, somewhere between 5–10 per cent of the French population today.

They are French-speaking and French-educated, but socially separate. They are still Muslim and they cannot easily assimilate. In 2004, the banning of head covers in the French public school system outraged the world.

The French seemed to be condemning their Muslim population. Yet few reporters noted that all Christian icons of religious belief in French public schools have been banned for decades.

Such a large and distinct population of French 'outsiders' in the urban centres, particularly in the public housing projects (*cités*) of Paris, has bred resentment among the more xenophobic of the French population, and resentment as well from the unassimilated.

While you will find many fascinating and culturally distinctive neighbourhoods—the Marais (1st) home to the Jews of France for centuries, the 13th with a large Asian community, the 19th and 20th and their neighbouring suburbs with the Blacks and Beurs—be aware that all is not rosy. The French still have some racial issues to sort out among themselves.

The young people of France, no matter what their origins, enjoy equal education and opportunity, up to a point.

HOW THE FRENCH SEE...

There are more than 70 million visitors to France each year, more than the entire population of the country. So the French are used to tourists. It may take you a little time to establish your uniqueness as the French have a few stereotypes of their own.

The French Canadians

The French embrace emotionally, if not economically, a large group of former colonies. If you are French Canadian, your accent will open the way to a warm, brotherly welcome. You are part of that global French family that it has been their mission to civilise.

Even the English-speaking Canadians enjoy special treatment from the French. They don't mind so much that you don't speak their language properly. Neither do the French Canadians.

Tolerance for Extremes

The French take pride in extending asylum to all those with radical ideas found unpopular elsewhere. Both the Ayatollah Khomeini and the Shah of Iran have been welcomed in France during their bouts of unpopularity at home. While France is a conservative country, she is highly tolerant of extremes.

The Americans from the USA

An American from the USA, as opposed to a Canadian, is different. No, he is not disliked by the French, contrary to the conclusion to which so many Americans jump. Even with the French opposition to the recent war in Iraq, most French people like Americans.

Americans are often considered conformist by the French, yet the French young emulate our dress code (running shoes, blue jeans and backpacks). American tourists generally eat too much, talk too loudy and dress sloppily.

Being an American myself, I can't see my own weaknesses well, but I am certainly quite sensitive to those of my countrymen. To the French, Americans are naive (easy pickpocket victims) and endlessly interested in how people make money and in how much everything costs, which are two taboo subjects in French conversation. (More on French etiquette to come.) They also have weak family ties, resulting in unstructured and haphazard lifestyles.

Many French people complain that Americans quickly become boring because they like everything superficially and yet understand nothing in great depth. Enthusiasm is not so admired in France as thoughtful analysis.

Yet basically, the French like Americans. They supported our revolution from England, so we are old friends. They respect our enthusiasm (in moderation), our cleverness and our energy. The French young dress and act like American film and rock stars. But they don't understand why Americans so quickly want to be friends.

The British

Migrations and conquests between France and England date back to the Celts, and probably earlier. They are still squabbling, though they did stick together in both of the last century's World Wars. Even with a healthy percentage of common blood, much is made by both sides about the peculiar differences between the Anglo-Saxons and the Gauls.

Stereotyping among the French paint the British as cold, insensitive, perfidious and stingy, with no sense of passion. An English person will invite you to dinner once, they say, then never again. (A French person may take a year to invite you, but after that, they will include you forever in their circle. More on this later.)

The Channel tunnel, the Eurostar service, has certainly brought these two nations closer together. It is only three hours now between London and Paris. But the enthusiasm remains lopsided. Over 12 million Britons visit France each year. Only three million French go to Britain. If nothing else, this indicates a clear consensus regarding the superiority of French cuisine.

One English person has been cheerfully adopted by France in recent years, the record-breaking round-the-world solo sailor Ellen MacArthur. The French are the best solo sailors in the world. The English say it is because no one will sail with them.

The Anglo-Saxons as Defined by the French

'...People talk about 'Anglo-Saxon' values, 'Anglo-Saxon' multinationals, 'Anglo-Saxon' consulting firms, legal practices, films, food, fashion and more...'

'American Democrat Jesse Jackson and filmmaker Spike Lee are called 'Anglo-Saxon' in France. The expression does not mean WASP. The concept has nothing to do with race or religion.
It refers to anything that comes from the United State, Great Britain, Australia, New Zealand, or Canada, but also Germany, Scandinavian countries like Denmark, even South Africa. What these countries share is a strong Protestant ethic, with a strong emphasis on community life, individual liberties, and economics.'

'So why don't the French just say Protestant? That would be admitting they are 'Catholic'. France is officially secular, and ever since the Church openly opposed democratic regimes from 1789 to 1944, 'Catholic' has been a dangerous word.'

—From *Sixty Million Frenchmen Cant be Wrong*

Australians bear that Crocodile Dundee image in France, as I assume they do nearly everywhere else. More often they are confused with loud, large and playful Americans, than with cold and stingy Brits. The French rarely pick up the difference in accent. Heavy drinking groups of young foreign men, however, win no points among the French. Even with a high rate of alcoholism, the French are intolerant of public displays of inebriation.

The Asians in General

Non-French Asians are generally assumed to be polite, very intelligent, hard-working and non-aggressive, except concerning money matters...similar to the French Asians.

Yet the Asian habit of keeping one's distance and not showing one's feelings (at least not in ways a French person can understand) can be interpreted as being cold and hypocritical. The Asian smile that springs of

Family Ties

The French share with most Asians their strong family connections. French writer Paul Morand compared the French and the Chinese in his book *Hiver Caraïbe* at the beginning of this century:

'There is a striking likeness between the Chinese and ourselves, the same passion for economy by making things last, by repairing them endlessly, the same genius for cooking, the same caution and old world courtesy, an inveterate but passive hatred of foreigners, conservatism tempered by social gales, lack of public spirit and the same indestructible vitality of old people who have passed the age of illness. Should we not think that all ancient civilisations have much in common?'

discomfort and embarrassment can be misinterpreted by a Frenchman as ingratiating.

Chinese cuisine, acknowledged even by the French as one of the world's best, helps the status of Asians generally in France, even though most Chinese food in France has been adjusted (to its detriment in my opinion) to accommodate the French preference for wine with meals. Vietnamese and Cambodian dishes marry the two far more successfully.

The Japanese

Until the Japanese started coming to France in great numbers in the 1980s and spending a great deal of money on French luxury goods, few French people distinguished among different Asian peoples. Japan is now the number one market for the best French food, wine, fashion, perfume, jewellery and technology. Japanese tourists are ubiquitous in the most elegant shopping districts of Paris and Japanese is widely written and spoken, at least well enough to close the deal.

There is both a fascination and a worry in things Japanese. French intellectuals love Japanese aesthetics: movies, literature and traditional arts, yet the Japanese reputation for copying technology and endlessly taking photographs is suspect. The way they flock to Japanese restaurants in Paris is also suspicious to the French. However, the Japanese are considered hard working and dignified, especially in their Gucci shoes and Chanel suits.

Other Cultures in General

Though many other cultural stereotypes exist, this is getting boring. A Frenchman will try to establish a relationship with you as an individual, if you gain his respect. As we delve more deeply into the fascinating complexities of the French, we hope to get you and them beyond these superficial stereotypes. We are past the skin of the onion and on to the meat of the matter.

BEYOND STEREOTYPES— FRENCH VALUES AND TRADITIONS YOU'LL NEED TO LEARN EARLY
French Bureaucracy in Your Life

In the 17th century under the reign of Louis XIV, his adviser Jean Baptiste Colbert centralised all power in the palace at Versailles. (The Grand Plan of French democracy described by Rousseau, quoted below, was already in the minds of the Parisians so the king decided to leave town.) The Napoleonic Code followed the example of Louis XIV and set a centralised approach into stone. Though power returned to Paris, today France still runs on the wheels of a massive bureaucracy in France.

Le Système D

Be on the lookout for le système D. The French take pride in their ability to Débrouiller bureaucracy, that is to 'untangle' it by resourceful means. There are many ways to do this, and you will learn the tricks as you go along. The best way is to have a friend who knows someone. Ask your French friends for help.

The French are accustomed to filling out endless forms, keeping mountains of records and giving the government information on every detail of their lives, all of their lives. Whether you are getting a driver's license or trying to find a job, you will be dealing with the unique and complex bureaucracy that is France. It will try the patience of Job, but don't give up, there is method in the madness.

The French complain about the hours of waiting in line and difficulty of getting answers from French bureaucrats. Just take

'Men are born and remain free and equal in rights.'
—Jean Jacques Rousseau

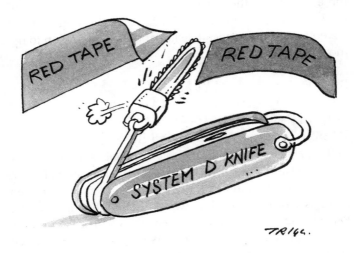

three deep breaths, expect many detours and bring some good reading material along to read while you are waiting.

Women's Rights

You will note that Rousseau's quote at the beginning of this section refers to the rights of 'men', not of 'people'. The original Napoleonic Code gave few rights to women. It is only since 1923 that women have had the right to open their own mail and only since World War II that women have had the right to vote.

However, French law protects women in many ways. The Government provides maternity and child care as well as abortion on demand. After a protest by anti-abortion groups in France, the manufacturer of the world's first legal 'abortion pill' took their product off the market. The French Government made them put it back on, arguing that it was an important medical advance for French women.

A woman alone with children holds all rights and obligations for the family, unless it is decided differently by the courts. Women who have a third child are rewarded with extra home-help allowances. But marriage and courtship are more formal and both marriage and divorce procedures more complex. A woman keeps her maiden name all her life, legally. She votes and pays taxes under that name, but rarely uses it socially.

The Transplanted Woman

Gabrielle Varro has lived in Paris for 35 years and is author of a book about international women, like herself, married to French men. *The Transplanted Woman* examines a number of the problems of intercultural marriages and multicultural children. She says that knowledge of the Napoleonic Code is essential for understanding the status of men and women in France. Although new laws regarding marriage and the rights of women came into effect in the 1970s, cultures change at a slower pace. Women can expect to be treated differently in France, both legally and culturally.

The role of women in the workplace is still fairly conservative. While small, entrepreneurial family businesses thrive, and women (wives) are very much involved, the man is still the head of the family. Male authority carries through into the corporate world. There are growing numbers of exceptions to this rule and in principle the French believe in the equal rights for women.

In reality, though, both women and men celebrate the differences between them. This enthusiasm for the opposite sex helps balance out the power structure better than any equal rights laws could. The French make an important distinction between 'sexy' and 'sexist'.

In 2000, a law was passed requiring all political parties to present equal numbers of men and women as candidates. The municipal elections in 2001 increased the participation of women to 33 per cent.

The Fonctionaire: Patience and Respect

Government workers (*les fonctionnaires*) and employees in large government-run organisations represent 40 per cent of the population of France today. In a world so centralised, you are going to meet a lot of these people and you must learn how to work with them.

These people don't have much status in the hierarchy, but they have great job security. They don't have to be nice to anybody. On top of that, they deal with a lot of argumentative French people. So they wouldn't tend towards warm and fuzzy, even if that were the normal French approach towards strangers.

Your patience is essential. You may have other things to do, but they do not. Walk into a post office telling yourself you have all the time in the world. Relax yourself in the queue by observing the people around you. Mimic how they deal with the situation.

Flee Boredom

The French love to argue, or rather, to debate. They call it 'discussion', and they have been doing it a long time. The Roman Tacitus reported that if the Gauls hadn't quarrelled so much among themselves, they wouldn't have been defeated. This quarrelling (the *engueulade*) has a healthy and positive direction to it. It brings a lot of ideas out onto the table to consider.

And the French don't always argue. To see the warm and fuzzy 'chick' inside the Gallic hot-and-cold rooster, take a puppy for a walk on any street in Paris. That aloof, elegantly dressed French woman will drop to your feet to slobber gurgles of adoration on the animal. She may be nearly as sympathetic with a human being, if he is on crutches (I only discovered this by breaking my leg.)

These strong shifts of mood and temper have a wonderful effect in France: they keep everyone from getting bored. More than anything, a Frenchman hates to be bored.

"Flee boredom," advised Coco Chanel. "It's fattening."

"They cannot bear being bored," said Alphonse de Lamartine of his countrymen in 1847. And they rarely are. Nor will you be..

When your turn comes, approach that fellow at the post office or the woman at the bank as a human being in an important professional capacity, whose assistance means a lot to you. (That is true.) Remember to say *Bonjour, Madame* or *Monsieur* first and try to have your questions ready in advance in proper French. Maintain their dignity and you will establish yours.

Since this book was first written 15 years ago, I have noticed a distinct sweetening of people in the service sector in France. Even the postal workers will give service with a smile sometimes.

Perhaps it is because I am getting older, which happily garners respect in France. Perhaps they have had a 'be nice to the tourist' campaign that I missed. But people seem more helpful in Paris now.

Whatever you do, don't ingratiate yourself, presenting a big smiley face. The French will worry that you are either a bit simple-minded or seriously deranged.

Disaster: A Happy Face

The French do not walk down the street smiling. Their politicians don't usually even smile for photographs. If a stranger smiles at you, he is trying to pick you up. If you smile at him, it is assumed you are doing the same. A person just walking along with a big wide grin on his face is assumed to be simple-minded.

I know. This is tough. All that beauty surrounding you on a bright autumn morning in a Paris park and you aren't allowed to smile? Yep.

You should smile politely when you say *Bonjour, Monsieur* inside a shop. You can smile at a cute baby or a dog in the park. But in general, to be considered an adult, you should exhibit reserve in public. Hold yourself up and remain a little aloof, hinting that you are also gracious, sincere and reasonable.

The 'No' Syndrome

Far less enviable than government workers are the retail shop workers in France. They are poorly paid, have little job status and less job security. Their predicament can breed resentment. They just might decide to play the 'put-down' game first and fast, before you can.

My favourite challenge in France is what I call the 'no' syndrome.

One of greatest quandaries of language is the meaning of the words 'yes' and 'no'. In Asia, some people say 'yes' and mean, 'yes, I heard your question' and then they think silently about the answer. This confuses Westerners, who think that their 'yes' means agreement. In the East, they are more anxious to avoid confrontation with an agreement than to answer the question right away.

In France, people will sometimes say 'no' even before you finish your question. This 'no' could mean: "That's not my job," or "I don't understand you," or "I'm busy now" or "I'm tired and can't think right now."

The Frenchman doesn't exist who is afraid of verbal confrontation. So no one is afraid to say 'no'. It is up to you to persevere beyond 'no'.

- First, take a deep breath. You have all the time in the world, right? Showing impatience means losing your cool. No Frenchman will respect that.
- Write down the name of the thing you want in French and practise saying it.
- Now, walk into the establishment and remember first and foremost to say *Bonjour, M...*, etc.) to whoever is working there. If the person sitting behind the cash register has no customers, you can ask her your question. If she is busy, continue on into the store and fine someone else who is free to listen. (Remember to say *Bonjour, M...* to the next person too.)
- If you get that pained 'Oh-god-what-awful-language-is-she-speaking?' grimace, try repeating your question a different way. Quietly. They aren't deaf, they just don't recognise your accent.

Getting the Item Without the Name

I had one delightful old fellow in a garden shop spend a full 15 minutes one day, figuring out the kind of plant seeds I wanted when the only name I knew for them was 'French Sorrel'. We discussed the leaf shape, the size and colour, the flavour, how it was eaten, if it had fruit. His face finally lit up and he said, "AH! Oseille!" and brought me right to the appropriate shelf of seed packets.

When I had asked him for "French Sorrel" he had said "no". But I knew he was bound to have them, so I explained that I didn't know the word in French, and it wasn't in my dictionary. By discussing the thing between us, he got it. He was as delighted as I was with our success.

MORAL: Barging into a shop demanding your wanted item is never the way to do business in France.

- If you have to, show the word from the dictionary to the store clerk. That should do it. "Ah, this person really wants my professional help!" they will conclude. "She's even willing to struggle with her pathetic French. So THAT is what she wants. Let me help the poor thing." The French do have a code of honour that doesn't allow them to stand by when someone is really suffering. I've also found the older the employee, the more helpful they will try to be... probably because they own the place.

In general, the ways to get through to people in public services in France are:
- Start with *Bonjour, Monsieur* or *Madame*
- Be patient
- Be sincere but not ingratiating
- Study the vocabulary you need in advance
- Respect the person's expertise and ask for it
- Try to establish an intelligent conclusion to the dialogue

If you are stuck with a surly young lady who clearly failed her English exams, and she abruptly turns away from your query with a '*non*', thank her back politely (you can maintain your dignity if she can't) and go find someone else. Or better yet, just go look yourself. Large department stores like Monoprix have so few staff, it will often be up to you to find what you want on your own.

If you still can't find it or find someone else who can, the very last ditch approach is to go back to the first person and talk about something else entirely. It can be something else of interest in the shop, the discount price of something, the interesting utility of something. Once you get her paying attention, slip in that earlier question. Her face may now brighten with the answer. If she really doesn't have it, she will at least tell you where else in the neighbourhood to look.

Often you will discover she had exactly what you wanted all along. Why did it take her so long to admit it? Well, she was probably intimidated by having to deal with you. Once you established a relationship with a conversation, that made you equals and less threatening. Your poor French and her poor English have brought you both past that point of awkwardness that keeps the French in their shell. It could have been she was afraid of being embarrassed by her poor English. It could have been she doesn't know the inventory very well. It could have been she was just tired or depressed. You must not take the 'no' syndrome personally.

The Rudeness Game

The waiter's position is, "I am feeling (choose any or all) tired/insecure/pressured/bored and here is this stranger at my table. Groan! I have plenty of other regular customers to take care of today. This lady probably doesn't even speak French. I wish she would just leave my restaurant and go somewhere else." You can respond one of several ways:

- **Lose**.
  You can take it personally, feel uncomfortable and decide to leave, tail between your legs. Ha! The Weakest Link. You lose.
- **Draw**
  You can respond with: "You may feel tired/insecure/pressured/bored but I am here to get a little service, darn it. I demand to have this, this and this." With that, you must snap your demands, in good French, and never make eye contact. Usually, the waiter/clerk will stonily fill the order, but he won't get any friendlier. That's a draw. It requires excellent French and lots of energy on your part. The refusal to make eye contact can become a contest itself. I've seen

Toujour Bonjour

In France, to enter a shop, or even a street kiosk, without saying *Bonjour, Madame* or *Bonjour, Monsieur* to the proprietor or clerk in attendance, acknowledging them as another human being, is very rude. In England or America, this type of behaviour would be considered unusual, even a bit forward. It is an important habit to develop in France, no matter what your other limitations. Always say *Bonjour, Madame* or *Monsieur*. If you know the shopkeeper already, you should make eye contact and continue the conversation in French with something like *Ça va?* .

a waiter and a client in a restaurant go through the entire ordering procedure, each diligently avoiding even looking in the other's direction. Even when the client pointed at the menu the waiter kept his eyes averted. They managed to get through the meal, so I guess that means they both 'won', but what a hollow victory! And after such a testy relationship, I'd check my bill carefully, if I were the customer. The waiter gets 15 per cent already included in the total (*service compris*).

- **Win**.
Think: "I'm not going to be put down by you. I have time and patience and I am going to remain gracious and continue to ask for your help and advice. Perhaps you will quit this silly game. I am here for a valid reason and you are important to my success." Nine times out of ten, you will win with this position, even if your French is poor. The fellow's attitude will improve, as you have maintained his dignity as well as your own. He may even remember you with a smile (well, almost) next time you walk in. Try and see.

Don't Take it Personally

You won't always win the rudeness game in France. It helps to keep your feathers well-oiled so the occasional insult can roll off your back.

No matter how badly you feel you are treated, if you have made your *Bonjour M...*, been patient and respectful (with eye contact) and the waiter or clerk still doesn't respond positively, just relax and resign yourself. This fellow is having a bad day.

NEVER take it personally. It is not you this person finds distasteful, but life itself. Keep reading this book, keep practising your French. You are going to learn how to tease that Frenchman into a smile, or even better, into a good discussion.

For the same reasons, no matter what transpires, or doesn't, never leave the shop without a *Merci, Monsieur* and *Au revoir, Madame* to these same people. You are acknowledging them as your 'hosts'. You are in their domain, their private space, and you must respect the relationship that exists between you by the mere fact of your being there, even if you are 'just looking'.

FITTING INTO THE FRENCH WAY OF LIFE

CHAPTER 4

'A lot of the peculiarities of French society,
including their obession with food, can be traced
back to the relationship the French have with
their land... The French word *pays* doesn't translate.
Literally, it means country. But inside France,
it refers to areas that are recognised as distinct...
There are hundreds of *pays* in France... *Pays* are
the spiritual countries of origin of the French...'
—*Sixty Million Frenchmen Can't Be Wrong*

SHOPPING—THE PERPETUAL TEMPTATION

There's nothing like shopping in France. The shops of Paris, like those of Tokyo, are designed to seduce you. The displays are so tempting, the arrangements so fresh and the products so unique, you will quickly begin to fall into the old lure of 'price is no object'. Exactly what they had in mind!

Shopping in the expensive parts of Paris (the 1st, 2nd, 7th, 8th and 16th *arrondissements*) gives a new meaning to the old term 'value for money'. The new 1 euro coin may be about the size of an American quarter, but it is worth more than a dollar... and it doesn't buy as much.

The French discriminate to the point of infinity. Don't be surprised to find a French person recommending only one *pâtisserie* in the neighbourhood, when there are a dozen of them and they all look and smell equally tempting to you. My Paris friends think nothing of going all the way across town for their favourite ice cream.

Parisians are particularly picky about their food, as we will discuss in detail in Chapter Six. They moan all the time about the declining quality, yet the rest of the world gasps at their wonderland of options.

There are few bargains in France. You really must shop carefully and compare prices. Generally I still consider food, wine and house wares 'a bargain' in France. That old French concept of craftsmanship still exists and is reflected well in these products. But you do need to shop around.

The Engueuelade

The French love to talk and especially to debate different points of view. They don't mind getting heated about it, either. A common approach to dialogue in France is the *engueuelade*, or roughly, bickering.

Not really argument, it starts with a cool, neutral approach. It is often used to establish the intentions and abilities of both customer and client, and can lead to mutual respect and trust, handled properly. It can also get very heated, but the goal is always an airing of ideas.

I once watched a half hour's conversation in a bicycle shop on the merits of two different bicycle tires. It was a very serious discussion and they seemed to bicker about the silliest details about each tire, even raising their voices over it. As I was waiting for the shopkeeper's attention myself, I had to listen to all this and I became a bit exasperated. But I waited my turn patiently and tried to pick up as much of the French as I could.

Finally, the tire was chosen and purchased and my turn came. The shopkeeper, an Englishman who has lived in France a long time, apologised for keeping me waiting. I couldn't help wondering out loud, in English, about the practicality of taking such a length of time so many joules of energy to sell a single tire.

"Yes," he agreed, a little frazzled himself, "but I wouldn't want him to buy something without considering all the options."

That's it in a nutshell. And from an Englishman!

MORAL: The French will usually want a thorough discussion before proceeding.

The French shopper has fine-tuned his or her skills to such a degree that if I see a crowd of people at a shop or stall, I get in the line. Even if I don't need chocolates or apples or new dinnerware that particular day, I know I'm going to get something rare in France: a bargain. Either that, or they simply sell the best chocolates/apples/dinnerware in Paris and it is a great value, no matter what the price is.

The only prices controlled in France are for basic bread (*la baguette*) and pharmaceuticals. To get your bargain 'fix', you might try the delightful discount 'dollar' shops all around Paris, full of things you didn't need but can't resist buying 'just for fun'.

They'll get you, those magnificent French retailers! You WILL consume! Read on for some of the basic rules you should know, if not follow.

Queueing

The French understand perfectly well the concept of lining up and being served in order. However, there is in France a curious desire to resist following the rules. It's part of the way people express their 'uniqueness'. And the French concede that an imaginative person will always have a good reason to break the rules.

So when someone breaks the queue, or smokes where it is forbidden, or parks in a no-parking spot, well, let him go ahead. The first time you need to take advantage of this flexibility you will appreciate it!

Dealing With Money and Getting Bilked

In many shops and in the markets, you will experience the French system of paying. It seems quite inefficient, but is a reflection of the French ambivalence towards money.

You inspect the products and make your choices with one shop person, who then gives you a ticket. You take this to the cashier. But don't try to hand this person the money. Instead, put your coins or credit card down on the little mat or counter intended for it. Take your change, your receipt and then collect your goods. Sometimes you have to return to the original sales clerk to get the goods. Even the modern department stores retain this two-step approach.

Tourist Hoaxes

There is a common hoax around the major tourist areas like the Louvre and the Eiffel Tower. A fellow pulls up in a nice car and asks if you are English/French/German/Japanese. He will be quite multilingual but look desperate and offer you his 'genuine Italian leather coat', any number of products, which he is holding in an otherwise empty car. It will always be the case that he is suddenly short of cash (he left his wallet at home, his wife drained the bank account, etc.). He just needs money to buy gas to get home, or to work, or something. He will literally give you the shirt off his back in exchange. The French love drama. Applaud the performance and keep walking.

Why? Well, first, this allows the person waiting on you to be more personable, to present the products to you without regard for price, free of the unpleasant necessity of taking your money. It also allows the boss to control the till. Usually the cashier is more senior than the service personnel. Usually it is a woman and often she is the owner or co-owner with her husband.

Money exchange is a tedious but serious thing in France. It should not distract from your shopping experience, but it should be in the hands of someone senior, an adult with wisdom and authority.

You will find a strong sense of honour among shoppers in France. Products are often out in alluring display on the sidewalk, whenever the weather allows, while the shopkeeper is inside attending to customers. I've never seen anyone shoplift anything, though it would be easy enough to do.

Count your change carefully and remember when you give a 20 euro bill instead of 10 euros that you get that extra 10 euros back! It's almost a game, giving incorrect change, and you are considered irresponsible if you let it happen to you. People check their bills and count their change in France. Money may be unpleasant, but it cannot be ignored.

Also watch for pickpockets, especially on busy market days, in crowds and in places where there are tourists.

Now, on to the variety of shops in France!

The Outdoor Markets

The open-air food markets of France are legendary and though a dying form of merchandising in the world, they are kept alive here by the vitality of both the products and the people who sell them. Bless their hearts.

All over France and all around Paris the old 'market day' tradition continues. Each neighbourhood has a regular *marché* street, set up at least once a week and each village will have a day when the merchants set up in the town square. Regular streets in Paris turn into block-long open-air bazaars. The most important market day is Sunday morning, when every French matriarch shops for the freshest goods for the most important meal of the week, Sunday afternoon. Her whole family will be gathered around the table.

Shopping here is quite different from going to the supermarket. You stand in line and wait your turn. Unless you see others doing it, don't pick up the products. You ask for *un* kilo of oranges (everything is metric: *le kilo* and *les grammes,* we can thank the French for this particular invention) and let the merchant pick them out. Some merchants now allow you to fill your own plastic bag directly from the display. But the more traditional guys will be offended if you do. They know they can pick the better ones.

Bring along a big canvas bag, a string bag or a wheeled cart to hold your various items. Once you become familiar with the way of doing things, you can start comparing produce quality and prices among the various sellers. You can establish good rapport with one or two of them. Then the fun of discovering unique or rare products and the day's best bargains begins.

I tend to cheat and use a universal short cut. I buy where I see the largest number of French women buying. Price haggling isn't done in these markets, at least not until around 1:30 pm when the merchants usually pack up for lunch themselves. Then, in order to get rid of perishable produce, they will mark down certain remaining items.

The Food Hawkers

The tide of humanity has opted for the predictability and convenience of giant department store and supermarket complexes in the international we-have-everything-packaged-up-and-sealed-for-your-protection-and-convenience mold.

Here is how Rudolph Chelminski describes the French antidote to such uniformity:

"These market food-hawkers are a very special race, both the men and the women: hangovers from the Middle Ages who mix commerce, theatre and social commentary in an ongoing chatter that is designed as much to amuse and entertain as to sell. Like *chansonniers*, the best ones can draw crowds when they are performing well. For some curious reason which I have never been able to fathom, the stars of the trade, the ones most thoroughly infected with *joie de vivre* (and, I suspect, *joie de boire*) are invariably the vegetable and fish people. Butchers are vastly more reserved, as befits millionaires, as are the B.O.F. (*beurre-oeufs-fromage*) ladies, silently dignified in their white smocks, and the tripe dealers—the offal organ grinders, as they are known around my house—tend to lurk in the shadows at the back of their sinister shops, amid their treasured collections of ears and snouts and lungs and intestines and pancreases and other unmentionables which the French know how to make edible. When a vegetable man is in good form, his voice and imagination fueled by a few litres of antifreeze, the merits of his radishes, celeries or artichokes become positively epic, possessing every virtue known to humankind and instantly available at a miraculous price, which would be even lower if it were not for those criminals who run the government."

—from *The French at Table*

Outdoor Markets

An important part of this outdoor entertainment is customer/seller exchange. Even if it's just a comment about the fruit, be sure to speak with that vegetable man. The variety and richness of a French outdoor market is positively sensual, and a flirtatious spirit pervades.

CREMERIE - EPICERI

Buying from traditional French shops, bring along a big bag for your purchases, and prepare to engage in conversation with the shopkeepers.

These merchants are professionals, in the true French sense. They love what they are selling and they love selling to people. Bring along your sense of humour as well as your appreciation of things French. Most of them open around 8:00 am, so you can come for breakfast and linger all morning.

The Speciality Stores

The first little shop that will draw you irresistibly inside will be *la pâtisserie*. Featuring fresh warm *croissants* from 7:00 am, an endless variety of beautiful sweet cakes, and some savoury pies and *patés*, they are a feast of the senses. At lunch, they may offer fresh sandwiches 'to go'.

Lord knows who consumes all of these delightful, fattening delicacies. Certainly not the skinny French. They are heavenly places no dieter would dream of entering. The *boulangerie* will specialise in those long *baguettes* of Paris, baked fresh twice daily, in early morning and early afternoon, as well as Sundays. No French person has to be reduced to consuming half-day-old bread.

You needn't even look for a *pâtisserie* or *boulangerie*. You will smell them. If the weather is at all decent, the shopkeepers wisely leave their doors open, cooling the bakery room and sending tempting wafts of fresh bread out to potential customers. Pure seduction. Better buy before 1:00 pm, though, as they also close for lunch.

Next to marvel upon must be the fish (*poissonnerie*) and meat (*charcuterie*) shops. Rudolph Chelminski has another quotable passage in his book on the *charcuterie* in France:

'... the *charcuteries* rank along with the wheel, gunpowder and Catherine Deneuve as fundamental contributions to civilisation. Literally, the word refers back to the cookers of meat—in medieval French, *chaircuitier*—but in modern terms it has come to mean a very special kind of artisanal food shop halfway between a butcher, where everything is raw, and the grocery store or supermarket, where everything is cooked, canned, conserved and industrially embalmed in one way or another. The *charcutiers* are more cooks than grocers, and what they sell is meant to be taken out and eaten at home or in the office. All of them offer the usual selection of cooked and smoked hams, of course, and sausages and cold cuts and pickles and even some canned and dried goods, but the heart of the *charcuterie* is in the dishes which the patron has cooked up fresh for the day: the whole chickens roasting on the *tournebroche* out on the sidewalk; the vats of the sidewalk; the vats of the peculiarly bland French version of *sauerkraut*; the pork and veal roasts, and the *rosbif* French style, so rare that the middle is hardly cooked at all. Around these staples, artfully arranged in the front window and then behind display counters inside, are several cornucopias of salads, cold *omelets*, smoked salmon, scallops on the half shell with *béchamel* sauce, decorated with little crescents of *pâte feuilletée*: these and a score of other delicacies, all of them sultry and seductive and ready to go home with the first customer who addresses them a kind word and a small bank note. A *charcutier's* front window display is enough to make grown men weep with pleasure and anticipation. I always carry a handkerchief myself, just in case.'

You probably won't need a handkerchief, but do carry something to haul home all the goodies they offer. (I carry those wheeled bags we older ladies in France are famous for.)

The Grands Magazins
The big fancy French department stores, Printemps, Galeries Lafayette, Bon Marché and the rest, look very little different from Harrod's in London, Seibu in Tokyo or Saks Fifth Avenue in New York. They carry everything from house wares to toys, but the emphasis is on fashion and cosmetics, with few bargains.

Catering to visitors, they offer money changing services, export discounts, a travel agency, theatre ticket sales, and multilingual staff. Good places to go when you want to avoid culture shock.

For better prices, try the ubiquitous monolithic discount stores in France, both national and international: Monoprix, Carrefour, Ikea, etc. Better prices but less French charm.

My favourite for price and selection in household goods is the BHV (*Bazar de la Hotel de Ville*), which has a fabulous hardware department in the basement, and lighting and furniture departments upstairs. Like the *grands magazins* they still feature cosmetics on the ground floor. They will deliver your purchases home, for a small fee.

Shopping For Non-French Specialities

No matter how good you are at coping with another culture, everybody wants to taste something from home, from time to time. Although most international restaurants in France have been adapted to French tastes, you can find more authentic ethnic food shops in the areas where those people live.

- Middle Eastern food   19th and 20th arrondissements
- American food   the 7th and 6th and Champs Elysée
- British food   the pubs, or Marks & Spencers near l'Opéra
- Chinese food   13th and 20th
- Greek food   in the 5th
- Indian food   Gare du Nord area
- Italian food   pizza places all over
- Japanese food   near l'Opéra, on rue St. Honoré
- 'kosher' food   the Marais

DRESSING THE CHANEL WAY

"The French are full of flattery for themselves," Coco Chanel once said. Some people criticise the French, especially the Parisians, for their overwhelming concern for the way they look. Indeed, there is something of the 'peacock' syndrome in Paris. (Remember that rooster.) People dress to show off, to display their taste and sense of class.

Tourists dressed sloppily and poorly groomed stick out like a sore thumb in Paris. If you want to feel like you are part of the scene, take a few basic lessons from your hosts.

The French are not frivolous about their street clothes. Chanel herself wore her suits seven or eight years (lacking dry cleaners, she then progressed to her line of perfumes). She chose materials that would last for 20 years.

"Elegance," she said, "is the contrary of negligence." Today you will still see her little black dress, her classic suits and bobbed haircuts, from Paris to Hong Kong to New York. She even instigated the fashion for a healthy tan.

The Parisians do nothing so well as dress, and it doesn't require a huge wardrobe. A woman or man might own only two or three basic outfits, but each will be the best quality and fit perfectly. They will feel great in them and that shows. Women use scarves and jewellery to make themselves endlessly original and fresh. Men can make a single fabric, a tie, a shirt, look polished.

Paris is still fairly formal. You won't find a professional French man or woman in jeans or running shoes. Only tourists and the young. Nor would a French woman dream of wearing shorts in Paris, though she calmly sunbathes nude on the beach.

One heartening thing about the French sense of fashion is that it knows no age. The youth syndrome less is pronounced here. Style and elegance are the domain of the experienced. "You can be irresistible at any age," Chanel said. "You have

Dressing Hints

For women
- Choose dresses, suits, skirts and blouses or well-fitted pants in dark or neutral colours. Limit whites and bright colours to one or two items: a scarf, a blouse, a sweater. Wear dress shoes or boots, preferably dark, that are comfortable for walking. An umbrella and overcoat for rain.
- In winter, have a well-cut wool, leather or synthetic coat, dark or neutral, to go with everything, that resists rain and wind. Carry a purse big enough for your essentials, which closes firmly against pickpockets. Carry a second fold-away bag for parcels. If you must carry a backpack, get an adult-looking one and don't put anything valuable in the zip pockets.

to replace youth by mystery. Elegance is the prerogative of those who have already taken possession of their future."

To dress well in Paris reflects taste and class. BCBG. (*Bon Chic, Bon Genre*) is a term the French use for what is stylish. The French don't slouch. Yes, the young like to imitate the relaxed American look, but everyone likes to look 'put together'. Parisian women know how to walk with confidence, turn with style, then sit and cross their legs provocatively. The men turn smoking a cigarette into a tantalising gesture. You don't have to be young and beautiful or even thin (though it helps). The French know how to capitalise on the beauty within, and so can you.

Nudity

Ironically, along with their high sense of fashion, the French also have a notorious lack of modesty. They bathe at public swimming pools and beaches in the nude. Men and women sunbathe along the banks of the Seine in summer, either nude or stripped to well below the waist. In spite of good public toilet facilities, men still urinate on the street.

Don't be shocked. Like the Japanese, the French don't recognise the sinful aspect of nudity. Join them if you wish, but don't misinterpret such nudity as an invitation for sexual advances. You'll get a sharp rebuff. Nudity in France is another form of fashion.

- Make sure your hair is well-groomed. (A haircut in Paris is a good way to start.) And don't overdo it with makeup.

For men
- Wear good wool or corduroy pants in winter, well-cut, with a belt. Heavy wool sweaters under your wool or leather jacket will help keep you warm in rain or wind. A 'macintosh' over everything and an umbrella will be useful. Leather moccasins or dress shoes are preferred, though more sporty shoes are acceptable now.
- In the countryside, the code is less formal and on the beach, it's less altogether.

Many who come to live in Paris pick up this fashion-and-style consciousness. I've seen women I would have pegged instantly as Perfect Parisians, only to discover as I get closer that they are speaking English with an American accent.

A great part of the drama of street life in Paris is admiring this continuously pleasant fashion spectacle. You can't help trying to emulating it.

NON-VERBAL COMMUNICATION

Fashion is one kind of non-verbal communication. It says quite a bit about how you see yourself. And the French have a critical eye for this. They also have many other ways of expressing themselves without words. This is a language you can pick up quickly.

Eye Contact

Making eye contact is a serious statement of equality in France. It invites a dialogue and so is too personal for strangers you pass on the street. (Unless, of course, you have some need to establish contact, like asking directions.)

There is a double standard to this. A woman who looks directly into a stranger's eyes in a public place is making a request for further intimacy. A man has the 'right' to toss a look at a woman whom he finds attractive. French men do it often. French women expect it.

Polly Platt calls this 'the Look' in her book *French or Foe?* and every woman who comes to France quickly becomes aware of it. Take it as a compliment, but don't return it. Don't even smile as you instantly look away.

Refusing to make eye contact gives you distance and control. (This is a favourite trick among French drivers: ignore the other car and he has to assume you didn't see him, and give you right of way.) But refusing to make eye contact with someone you are dealing with directly is an insult. Establish at least some brief eye contact with people who are supposed to be helping you. You will get far better service.

Shaking Hands

The French shake hands with everyone they know, unless they kiss them, instead (*see* The Double Kiss). It's not a strong handshake, as in the 'gripper' American-style, with a long, serious moment of eye contact. It's a brief holding of the hands with an even briefer visual acknowledgement, but it is essential as a French greeting among colleagues.

Children are taught to shake hands from the time they can walk. You will soon become accustomed to the handshake, and soon be able to imitate the lightness of touch and eye-contact required. When you do get into a handshaking situation yourself, whether at work or in social situations, be sure not to exclude anyone in the group, even if you don't know them.

In an office environment, you will be expected to shake hands both in the morning and at the end of the day, with all the other staff.

A Smile

If you are American, this is going to be your single biggest non-verbal miscommunication when in you are in France. The tendency of Americans is to smile all the time. In America, it makes us appear friendly and reasonable. The French do not trust a smile. If they can see no apparent reason for it, it appears idiotic (very unreasonable) or hypocritical, a very unpleasant thing to a French person.

There is a wonderful example of this in Polly Platt's *French or Foe?* where she recalls showing some French executives a picture of their then President Mitterrand at an informal meeting in Texas, smiling. Nobody recognised him! He never smiles for the cameras in France, or at least those shots are censored by the French press.

As a Californian, I smile automatically. I look better when I smile and I feel better. But in France I have to constantly remind myself to wipe that smile off my face as I walk down the street, so happy to be in Paris. It makes people nervous. Am I an idiot, they wonder? Am I laughing at their expense?

While I love France and I really love being there, I know that a constant smile on my face will not convey my appreciation.

More important, you never smile at a stranger on the street and say 'hello' just to be friendly. If a construction worker whistles at you or a stranger gives you 'the Look' or a street person asks you for money, your lack of expression keeps the situation neutral and dignified. It is your best response.

Don't get me wrong—you can smile a lot when in France. But not at strangers and not just to yourself. The French love to smile, and do so very quickly, when there is a good reason.

The Reverse Kiss
The French make a 'poof' sound, at the same time blowing air out of their mouth and protracting their lips. That means 'it's nothing', either negative or positive, depending on the situation and context. It is a very popular expression. Sort of the opposite of a smile.

The Double Kiss
Between friends who are greeting or parting, a kiss on both cheeks is normal, even in public. Again, if there is a group, you should be sure to kiss everyone, even if you don't really know them, treat them as equal among those you do know.

Teenage schoolgirls greeting each other with a double kiss.

Don't panic. This is not usually expected in business and certainly not between businessmen, only between women, between men and women, between adults and children and between men who are members of the same family.

The Circular Handshake

At first, it can be most aggravating, this business of shaking hands with everyone, especially in the office and or at the bank. Go to your bank first thing in the morning as they are opening and you will watch an endless round of handshake greetings amongst the bank staff . I stood and waited helpless one morning, hoping at some point my teller will be able to free his hands and attention long enough to get on with my request and his job. But this is part of his job! Each employee is obliged to make a handshaking round to every other employee both on arrival and on departure. In a small office with 20 employees... that's 800 handshakes each day! Comparing such counterproductive formalities with the rush to serve customers in places like Hong Kong, one wonders how the French have managed to retain fourth place among the world's strongest economies.

This is a tough one for those of us not accustomed to facial contact with anyone save our most intimate circle. I find myself more comfortable with this exercise the longer I stay in France and have tried to carry the habit home with me, with some success. Among women, particularly, it is a fun little expression of affection, once the technique is perfected.

Start with the right cheeks touching. If the other person seems bound and determined to go for the left cheek first, for heaven's sake make that one available instead. Otherwise you may smash into each other's mouths, a painful and embarrassingly intimate error.

Most foreigners, myself included, have reduced the intimacy of the double kiss by 'kissing the air', instead of actually touching lips to cheek. Anatomy only allows one mouth in contact with the other's cheek anyway. So most of us let the French friend make that contact, if they choose. Many French also use this 'kissing the air' technique.

Two kisses is the minimum. Three, alternating cheeks each time, is shows further intimacy and is not unusual in Paris. Parisian women will even extend it to four with their women friends, which to me is gilding the lily.

Whole Body Language

French women and men, especially Parisians, have a reputation for being stunningly good-looking. In fact, they are not, at least by Hollywood standards. Their skin may be poor or their teeth bad. They may look tired around the eyes and many French women never bother with make-up.

What gives the French an aura of beauty is the way they present themselves. They hold their bodies erect and they are conscious of themselves as extensions of their whole personality. Like actors, they make their bodies convey whatever message they feel appropriate. The usual messages are: "I am intelligent/sincere/well-raised." In this way, they convey an inner beauty.

It doesn't hurt, of course, that some Parisians are horrified by the prospect of getting fat and diet religiously and walk everywhere, so they do look good in the beautiful and expensive clothes they wear. But others convey elegance and a refined sense of themselves in properly cut jeans.

Few French people are more than vaguely aware of this powerful performance their body language presents. This proper carriage and the importance of presentation is taught at an early age and is everywhere apparent. It is second nature to the French to look good.

Non-verbal communication, a whole body language, was perfected by the French mime Marcel Marceau. His mimics are everywhere.

You will quickly become more conscious of the way you dress and how your body conveys messages. You will find yourself imitating in short order.

Come to France in clothes that make you feel good about yourself in the mirror. Walk tall. Reserve your smiles for people you deal with directly. You'll pick up the finer points as you go along.

Touching Distance

The French touch each other to express friendship rather than any physical desire. This is reserved for friends, of course, but close physical contact can be expected in crowded places in Paris, even among strangers. The French have learned to tolerate this with calm reserve, and so will you. Just watch for pickpockets in crowds. If a stranger purposely touches you, give a really nasty 'poof' or just ignore him completely, and get away as soon as you can, walking with your head held high.

Vocabulary of the Fingers and Hands

- When counting in France, 'one' is the thumb. The index finger and thumb extended together means 'two'. So putting up an index finger to mean 'one' is confusing to French people. Do you mean 'one' (the thumb) or 'two' (the thumb and index finger)?
- Don't ever snap your fingers at a person, anywhere. That is rude and condescending.
- One or several fingers circling at the temple means 'that guy is crazy' (*dingue*) and is usually accompanied by a goofy expression.
- Holding one's nose with the fist and faking a turn indicates 'that guy is drunk'. (*Il est saoul.*) A condition always to be ridiculed.
- Kissing the tips of one's fingers means 'delicious', whether it is the food at the table or a woman walking down the street.
- Pulling the right cheek downward at the eye, with the right hand means, 'I don't believe it'. (Literal: *mon œil* as in 'my foot'.)
- The 'OK' circle made with the tip of the thumb and index fingers touching means the number 'zero', or worthless. But some people now use it to mean 'OK', especially if accompanied by a pucker of the lips.
- Thumbs down—bad. Thumbs up means Super!
- The fingers flat against the lips with eyes open means, 'Oops, I made a mistake'. No verbal comment is necessary.
- Shaking the fingers of the right hand in front of the chest means great surprise and excitement, positive or negative, and is appropriately accompanied by an 'Ooh, la, la!'
- Raising the shoulders, the classic French shrug, this means 'This is ridiculous' or 'So what can anyone do?'

- Both hands up in front of the chest, palms out, with a shrug means 'I don't know' or 'Hey, it's not my job'.
- A hand wiped across the forehead or just above the hairline means 'I've had it up to here'. (*J'en ai ras-le-bol*)
- Using the back of the fingers to stroke the right cheek as if it were a beard means *Quelle barbe* or 'What a bore'.
- The finger tips rubbed together, with the thumbs up, as if one were feeling fabric, means 'expensive'.
- The fingers together, all reaching skyward, means 'I'm afraid' or 'he's afraid'. (Literal: 'Soft balls, we can feel them'.) With the reverse kiss, the 'poof', it is contemptuous commentary roughly equivalent to 'screw you'.
- The same 'poof' with a hand throwing something over the opposite shoulder means, 'It's nothing; I'm above this'.
- Making a fist with the right hand and stretching out that arm, then 'breaking' it at the elbow with the left wrist is equivalent, in other places, to raising one's middle finger. (*Va te faire foutre!* or 'Get stuffed!').
- Making a fist and shaking it leisurely in front of one's chest is often used by men to mean 'He's a jerk', and is really an imitation of 'jerking off'.

You will find many more of these colourful phrases with further observation. The French constantly speak with their hands and bodies. It is a wonderful part of their Mediterranean heritage and great fun to watch in public places. It is one reason why putting one's hands in one's pockets or even in one's lap at a meal is considered impolite. It denies conversation. Keep your wrists resting on the edge of the table.

THE FAMILY CYCLE OF LIFE

The French put family first. Family is the social cement and a specific, personal duty of each individual member. Outside are public life, philosophy, politics, art and cuisine. Inside is family.

Although French people can be very romantic about 'love', they take marriage and children in a very practical way. The extended family supplies emotional and economic support. Marriage is one building block of that extended family. It is not just something to fulfil one's personal needs. (Lovers are for that.)

However, as Raymonde Carroll notes, marriage is not the threshold into adulthood. Having children is. Children constitute the parents' obligation and link to the family and to the society at large.

Children are a joy to their parents, as they are in all cultures, but they also involve a serious burden of obligation to the respective families of those parents. (Asian readers will have an easier time understanding this than Americans.)

You Are Also a 'Child'

Being an adult is being a parent in France. The adult French person feels free to give instruction to anyone he considers in need of it, including a foreigner. You may find yourself being corrected quite directly for some error on your part, by a French person you never saw before in your life.

Don't feel insulted! Thank them for the compliment! This French person is actually extending himself to you with a generous spirit. He is paying you the compliment of giving his real 'parental' concern. Remember that duck's back! Say "*Merci, Madame!*" and make the correction.

Children

Children, in France, are seen as a reflection of their parents' duty to the family. Therefore, their proper behaviour, especially in public, is very important. Those old-fashioned ideas that children should be well-dressed and well-behaved, even notions that they should be 'seen and not heard' are still upheld in modern-day France, though it is getting harder to keep that standard up everywhere in the world.

Parents will reprimand their children in public, sometimes to show other adults that they are trying to do the job correctly and to really instruct the child. In public, in the absence of the

parents, other adults will quickly feel invested with parental responsibility. The French adore their children, but they show that affection with a firm hand and a serious purpose.

They are not playmates to their children, as in some other cultures. Their job is to civilise. The child seeks companionship among his siblings and other children. When there is an adult party at home, the children will usually be sent off among themselves, and they will be expected to work out their differences with the older children taking responsibility for the younger ones.

At adolescence, the isolation of childhood is ended, the rules are relaxed. Teenagers are rewarded with an apprenticeship into civilised society, with the freedom to experiment and explore. They are supported by their families and live at home, but each is allowed a remarkable degree

Children's Place

'The French don't regard childhood as an age of innocence, but see it as an age of ignorance. Children must be set straight and corrected. French parents are, on the whole, quite authoritarian about child rearing, and they teach their children to respect rules from a young age.'
—from *Sixty Million Frenchmen Can't be Wrong*

Laying Blame

While criticism is freely given in France, when it is needed, finding fault with someone is another matter. You do something wrong out of ignorance, you are corrected, like a child. Blaming someone for something already done, like a traffic accident, is taboo. Never mind who was at fault. The important topic should be how to resolve the situation.

Barlow and Benoît-Nadeau explain in their book:
'The term *faute* (fault) is very grave in the French mindset. 'Worse than a crime, it's a blunder!' were the famous words of diplomat Charles de Talleyrand (1754–1838). This thinking is one reason the French are loathe to admit being at fault for even the smallest mistakes, even in private.'

of independence, compared to many cultures.

Parents and other adults will still correct and criticise these teenagers, but they are generally allowed to go about their business. The 'control' at this point becomes the family bond. The child's conduct always reflects back on the parents and the child is aware of this responsibility throughout his life.

Teenagers are encouraged to participate in family discussions, to reason and to think for themselves. High school students are even allowed to smoke in France, and will go out with their teachers to a café.

Parents will continue to participate in their children's lives, of course, intervening on behalf of their children throughout the school years to university level and helping with that first break in the job world, but these children are not 'babied'.

Because of this respect for their independence, children who are not married often continue to live happily at home. "The French support their children until they are stepping on their beards," says one British friend who has lived in France most of his life.

When children marry, the parents will often help them out with housing, furniture and other expenses. After this, the cycle of care and belonging starts again when the young parents start their 'civilising' job with their own children. Childless marriages are rarely a goal.

Being a Couple

Though a young couple remains in the 'adolescent' stage until their first child is born, the relationship itself separates them in one important way from their world of friends. The

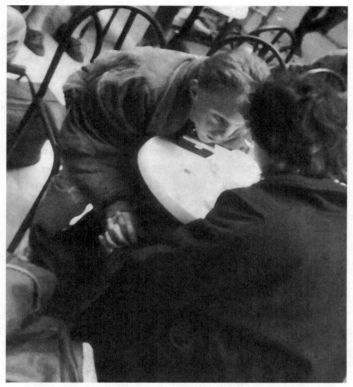

A guy acting like a child towards his girlfriend. Couples do appear childlike in France until their have their own children.

intimate details of their life together will not be subject for discussion. Passion and intimacy between the couple is reserved for the two of them, either at home or in a totally anonymous public situation (such as the classic Paris scene of a couple walking down the street locked in a kiss).

However, being a couple does not mean that they now do everything together and exclude their old friends. After the initial glow subsides, both in public and with friends, the couple will be expected to act in their normal, individual way, expressing their opinions, showing their emotions and maintaining their circles of relationship.

In company, one partner may criticise the other without reflecting on the status of the marriage. To show the special nature of the solidarity between them, they may make each

Enjoying the parks is a family pastime in France, locals and visitors alike.

other the butt of their jokes. Couples who argue issues when among their friends are considered to be acting normally, like individuals.

Harmony, which is an important public image for married couples in many cultures, can look like indifference to the French. It might even indicate boredom in the marriage. And we know anything, to the French, is better than being bored!

Ageing

As parents age, they slowly (and not without protest) switch roles, eventually becoming their children's responsibility. While the relationships between parents and children continue to be close, the goal here is not to be 'friends' with each other but to excel in their roles as parents and children.

(Friendships are a special category of relationships, as we will soon see.)

The parent/child role reversal can come quite early in life in France. When they reach 35, many young parents find their own parents already calling on them for advice and obeying their suggestions. As the French now prefer smaller families, they are also experiencing the nuclear family syndrome. Older members of the family retire and move away from children and grandchildren. Still, in France, the traditional Sunday lunch, with the whole family crowded together at the table, is still a 'command performance' wherever and whenever it is still possible.

Evidence of this is still clear in the parks of Paris, which will be nearly empty on a Sunday morning, as families prepare the noonday meal. After lunch, these parks will flood with family groups; all generations, strolling together, all dressed up and usually deeply involved in several conversations, bodies gesturing enthusiastically.

If a Sunday gathering is not possible, a long telephone call between parents and children is expected. (This 20th century invention has been adapted very differently, according to the French sense of private vs public, as we will soon see.)

Pets

A visit to any French market will convince you that the French love to eat all parts of all animals. Not true. Some animals, especially small dogs and cats, get better treatment than humans. English writer Fay Sharman, author of *Coping with France*, is horrified by this contrast:

'The French attitude to animals is a bizarre mix of brutality, indifference and adoration. They think nothing of shooting larks and thrushes or keeping live rabbits horribly cooped up at the market... they are altogether unsqueamish... Yet the French have suddenly become a nation of pet lovers.'

Dogs and cats bask in undeserved affection in France, especially in Paris. Owners cuddle them shamelessly. (They would never be so demonstrative with their own children.)

Strangers who would not give the owner a glance will drop to their knees to give their pet a smooch. It's a sad commentary (to me) on what is otherwise a dignified and logical culture.

On the street, in cafés, in shops, in restaurants, nobody seems to mind a perpetually yapping miniature poodle though a human being making an equal volume of disturbance would be arrested. The most obnoxious evidence of these indulged pets is their ubiquitous droppings that litter the otherwise stunning Paris sidewalks.

Visitors complain that you can't look up at the architecture because you're so busy looking down to avoid the dog poop. Pet owners ignore both the French 'pooper-scooper' laws that require them to clean up behind their animals and the white dog silhouettes painted on sidewalks that remind everyone to bring Fru-fru to the curb-side before he relieves himself. Indulgent Parisians remain tolerant of what thousands of little Totos leave behind. Yet they remark unkindly when Asian children are allowed to pee in the gutter in China.

Explaining French Inconsistency

The French love some small domesticated animals though they eat almost all the wild ones. They take tremendous pride in their beautiful Paris walkways, yet they let a poodle use it as a bathroom. Who can explain that? Well, our Sixty Million Canadians offer the best explanation I have found so far:

'In France, most of these (clean-up) responsibilities are shouldered by the state. It is easy to think the French are uncivil and inconsiderate, especially when they refuse to observe the basic courtesies like scooping up after their dogs. But people pay high taxes and expect the state to do its job. And the state does its job. The French don't have very rich community lives. But they do draw a limit on moralising individual behaviour. We found that there was a certain *liberté* to that.'

Only the Mayor of Paris seems worried. The city has a battalion of men and machines (called *motocrottes*) dedicated to keeping up with this single problem. While they work the pavements, other men in enormous green trucks collect city garbage every morning, including Sundays, and flood city gutters in strict schedules to keep the beloved City of Light clean. No matter. Pets keep the upper hand... er, leg.

The French, whose high taxes are paying for all this clean-up, have decided it is actually good luck to step in dog doodoo... a rather stoic approach to what is considered an avoidable nuisance in most urban environments. You will have to watch your step and walk with agility, especially in Paris, to avoid 'good luck'.

The Circles of Friends

Most French people establish friendships slowly. This is not because they are unfriendly, but because a friend is a serious commitment, an extension of one's family responsibilities in life. So be patient and don't try to push yourself on people.

Raymonde Carroll says that a friend in France is what you would expect: someone who loves you like a sibling, whom you can trust, whose company you enjoy, who accepts you as you are. Friends help each other, but in France, friends are expected to do more. They are expected to help guide, correct and participate in each other's lives.

Break A Leg

I had my first insight into the value of this French soft spot for pets when I became one. No, I wasn't on a leash. I was on crutches, having broken my ankle rushing too fast down the seven flights of stairs from my little *chambre de bonne*.

After nursing the swollen ankle for two days, my *guardienne*, who was keeping me supplied with hot soup and the mail, escorted me to a local clinic. I walked back out on the street with my torquoise coloured cast and matching *bequille* (crutches) to a different Paris.

French strangers stopped me to express their condolences and offer assistance. Four lanes of traffic would stop silently on a green light so I could hobble across the street. In the restaurants, the waiters rushed to clear my way to a convenient table. Everyone expressed their genuine sympathy.

In my building, neighbours who had never said more than 'Bonjour, Madame' in ten years suddenly offered to let me access my little servant's room via their apartment and their elevator. A taxi driver offered to take me to my cancelled appointment in Moscow, for free. (He said he'd always wanted to go, anyway.)

I was incredulous, but here's how I figure it: in becoming helpless, I became a pet, totally dependent on others. The French are remarkably attuned to that.

In the Gallic view, life is hard, cruel and ugly. It can be made to appear beautiful and pleasant and every step should be made to do so. That is why it is important to the French that things look so well, regardless of the chaos and deterioration the beautiful facade might cover up. But friendliness? Friendliness is reserved for those who merit the effort: family, friends and the helpless.

In a hard, cruel world, little pet animals are totally dependent on humans for their survival. They require our generosity. They cannot be taught to be tough, as children can; they can only beg for mercy. So it is with people on crutches.

The opposite was true when I got on the plane to go home. I took an American carrier. Boarding at Charles de Gaulle Airport, I got the typical American treatment of people on crutches. I was ignored, unless I asked specifically for their help.

My advice? Break your leg in Paris. Just remember to watch out for the dog droppings.

French friends are always talking on the telephone, always discussing their personal problems in detail and always planning events together. Yet the French will rarely analyse the relationship between the two of you.

They prefer to discuss other things, like politics, art, fashion and events. Such discussions lead to an exploration of difference points of view. Disagreements? Great. Your friendship will be enriched. You will be appreciated for being provocative and witty more than for just being supportive.

The French do not worry about being 'equal' with their friends. They do not count favours or seek an equilibrium in the number of dinner parties or gifts one presents the other. They expect their friends to love them as family and the activity of reaching out to each other is more important than remembering who reached further or first.

Carroll notes some interesting examples of this. A good friend calls another, saying she is exhausted. The friend immediately offers to come over, take the children, and allow her friend a few hours' relief. Pretty amazing, eh?

In France, friends can call on each other, day or night, for the slightest reasons. The telephone is an extension of their relationship, another visit, another chance to connect, and the conversations are rarely short.

French people will call each other, right after they get home from a party together, if they think of something they forgot to say, or they have a bit more news or analysis to offer. Between friends, a telephone is a line of love. When friends call you on the telephone, they will rarely introduce themselves, expecting you to recognise his voice (and thereby confirm yourself: if it wasn't you, you wouldn't know who they were.)

French friends often do things together several times a week. As you become friends with a French person, you can expect to be pulled into the close circle, meeting other friends, and be included in their activities.

You will also be expected to fulfil these myriad emotional obligations and commitments. That is why the expansion of the friendship circle is slow in France. Each of us has limited amounts of time and energy, so we must limit the number of people with whom we can be true friends.

Counting many people as 'friends', and therefore being very 'popular' is not the French ideal. It is quality rather than quantity that counts.

Compliments

French people are very conscious of their surroundings. You don't get cities like Paris or from countryside like the Loire Valley without making a lot of effort. The French take the impressions of other people seriously. They don't like false compliments.

Commenting on a pretty dress, a new pair of shoes or new haircut is a natural thing to do. But different cultures respond to this commentary differently. Americans are taught to say 'thank you' when they receive a compliment, implying, "Thank you for making note of me." These compliments are more polite than commentary.

In the East, a compliment is usually denied, meaning, "Oh no, I really am not that good. You are too kind and good to see how lowly I am." Compliments aren't usually given, just because they are awkward to receive.

The French make sincere compliments, not to be polite but because they really have an opinion. Your response should reflect your appreciation of their opinion.

Don't deny the compliment. That would be an insult. Just saying, 'thank you' is to imply, "Thank you, yes, I agree my dress is terrific." Quite pretentious. A proper reply is something like, "Oh, do you really think so? (with no sarcasm intended) I'm so glad you like it!" implying you appreciate and respect their opinion. And wear that dress more often!

BEING A GUEST IN A FRENCH HOUSE

You've been invited to a French home for dinner. BOY! Are you lucky! Few people, even French people, get such invitations. The French home is very private and very much family-oriented, as we have noted, so an invitation for dinner implies a high level of comfort with you and regard for you.

The size of Paris apartments, especially kitchens, limits the extent to which the French can comfortably entertain at home. Plus, expectations of the cuisine are so high, people usually prefer to go out.

This is something you can suggest to your French acquaintances. Never ask to visit someone's home if you haven't already been invited. If you need to stop by for some reason, telephone first.

Accidents Will Happen

If you should have an accident in your host's home, say you spill something on a rug or break a glass, you will be immediately reprieved. No matter how valuable the object, your host will toss off the loss as nothing worth considering. This is good manners in France. Friends are always more valuable than things.

Hosts accepts responsibility for guests as they would for their children. (Another reason, perhaps, why French people are slow to invite people to their homes!) Offer to replace or repair the damage, of course, but don't insist. You will probably be told that the Baccarat crystal goblet was 'really worthless'.

If you do break a valuable object, you might consider sending a nice gift, later, just to express your appreciation for your friends' generosity.

If you are not invited to a French person's home, don't feel offended. A century ago, Henry James complained that though he had been invited to the salons of Flaubert, and regularly met Zola, Maupassant and the other luminaries of the day (he also being well-known by then) they always treated him as if he were a total stranger, as if he weren't there.

He complained to his family, as he finally left Paris to live in London, "It is rather ignoble to stay simply for the restaurants," implying that he was never asked to French homes. But Henry James also said very positive things about his Paris life:

"You know, you get all ready to hate the French—it happens all the time when you live in Paris—then they'll turn around and say something or joke about themselves, and you like them all over again." Henry James had some cultural misunderstandings about the French he never sorted out. But you can.

BEING A GOOD GUEST

Once you are invited to a French home, remember these basic rules which the French also follow. They will help you get invited back and thus help you establish a friendship for life. That is how the French are about their friends.

- Arrive at the appointed time, but not earlier. Up to half-hour late is OK in the evening in a home, but not in a restaurant. You will probably be invited for 8:00 pm or later in Paris.

- Dress as you would go out to a restaurant for dinner, the later the appointed hour, the more fancy the dress code. For the men, the code rarely goes beyond a suit and tie.

- Don't arrive empty-handed. Bring a small offering, something from one of those delightful little speciality shops you've been admiring. Don't bring wine. (*see* Rules For Gifts *on the opposite page*)

- Allow time to find the address. The numbers on buildings in Paris increase very slowly. Number 20 may be a long walk from number 2, and often there is a 2b following number 2 and before number 4, all independent addresses. Don't forget to ask for the door code, as most residential buildings in Paris now have front doors that are locked. You punch the code into the key pad outside. A green light will come on, a click or a buzzer will sound, and the door unlocks. The individual doorbells in the building will be inside.

- You will be welcomed into the living room and offered an *apéritif*... called a 'cocktail', but it will probably be something small and sweet, or a short whisky. Don't have the *faute de goût* (bad taste) to ask for wine. Wines will be served with the meal. Let your hosts serve you. Stand to receive your drink when it comes and to greet other guests.

- There will be something to nibble, crackers or nuts rather than fancy American *hors d'oeuvres* (which on a restaurant menu usually means assorted vegetables). The meal may well be an hour or more away, but don't fill up. Polly Platt refers to this 'introductory' period of the French evening at home as a very awkward one. It is your job to help everyone relax. Tell a funny (short) story about an experience you've had in Paris, especially it gives an insight into your growing understanding of the French way of doing things.

- One thing NOT done in France during this 'warm-up' is a house tour. The French consider it 'showing off' to invite guests to see their home, and they won't be prepared for it. So, stay where you have been placed. Don't even follow your host or hostess into the kitchen to help. You can offer to help, but take your host's decline seriously. You are the guest and it is their pleasure to serve you. The only other

Rules for Gifts

- Give something on which the host would not usually indulge themselves in, something that appeals to the intellect or aesthetic, but nothing embarrassingly extravagant. Indulge yourself in one of the fine speciality shops of Paris.
- A present for each of the children is a good idea if you are going for a noonday meal and need a good distraction. For an adult dinner at a home, the children will only appear to greet guests, then disappear for the rest of the evening.
- Arranged flowers are a good choice. Avoid even numbers (bad luck),chrysanthemums and carnations (reserved for funerals), and red roses (reserved for lovers). Chocolates are an excellent choice, especially a small box of very good ones from a speciality shop, well wrapped. Most chocolate and flower shops will ask, when you buy, if your purchase is *pour offrir* (a gift). If so, they will wrap them accordingly.
- Unless you are in the wine business, or friends have specifically asked for it, avoid bringing wine. The wine, like the dinner, is usually an expression of the host's tastes and hospitality.

room in the house you are likely to see on this visit is the toilet (the WC, not the bathroom, usually two different places). Likewise, don't help yourself at the bar (unless instructed to do so) and don't investigate an interesting book on a shelf or object in a case more closely. You are there to be an interesting human being.

- To be incorporated into the small friendship circle of this French acquaintance, you have an important duty. You must participate in the conversation waltz, however you can. (*See* Chapters 6:Restaurants and Wine—The French Essentials *and* Chpater 8: Parlez-vousFrançais? *on pages 120 and 167 respectively.*)
- At table, you will usually be assigned a seat by the hostess, so look for name cards or await her command.
- Silverware is often placed downward. You should start with the pieces on the outside and work your way in. The pieces above your plate are for dessert. Often, another set of utensils will be served with the cheese. Each course will be served on new plates.

Living With a French Family

You've found a family to live with! Now you will see how truly warm and generous the French are. You will be treated like real family. Here are just a few preparatory thoughts.

- In addition to the points mentioned above, remember to respect the household privacy. Don't wander into rooms with closed doors without knocking first. Leave the toilet and bathroom doors closed.
- Don't help yourself in the kitchen unless instructed to do so. Ask before using the TV, stereo or even a radio. Do help out whenever possible with clearing the dishes and washing up.
- The French are very concerned about disturbing their neighbours. As a guest, be particularly concerned

- Wine will be served with the first course. Once everyone is served, the host may offer a toast to the guests or just a "*Salut!*". Don't start drinking before that. There will probably be several different wines, one for each course but the salad. The one unbending rule here is: don't drink too much!
- Try eating with your knife in the right hand and your fork in the left. It's the French way and very efficient, especially with salad.
- You may rest both arms on the table, between bites, but not elbows. Don't keep your hands in your lap.It implies you aren't going to join the conversation!
- Break your bread off from the main loaf, if it hasn't been cut already. Put the uneaten part or parts next to your plate, so they don't get soggy in the sauces
- Sincere comments about the food and the wine are always a good topic of conversation. (But guard against false compliments—worse than none at all in France.) In a restaurant, you can be critical of the food;

about this. For example, don't play your music loudly, or even bathe late at night. Don't speaking loudly in the building's public spaces.

- If you are a student going to live with a French family, do not assume that you are being accepted as an equal. You are a family member, but still a 'child'. Respect their rules and the private spaces in the home outside your own room. Don't let it all hang out unless behind the closed door of your own assigned space.
- Because there is little private space in France, your presence will be a major impact on each member of the family. Try to minimise that impact, wherever possible. That is the basis of what the whole world knows as 'good manners'.

at home, of course, if you can't say anything nice, don't say anything at all.

- Try to finish most of the food on your plate. It is a compliment to the hosts. The meals in Paris will be much lighter than those in the country, where your request for 'seconds' will be more appreciated.

- It is very tempting to soak up the delicious sauces in France with your bread. That is all right to do with company you know well, or if you see the host do it, but use your fork, not your fingers, to swirl the bread.

- When you have finished a course, put your silverware together across the plate, fork up. Leaving silverware opposing each other on the plate implies you are not finished.

- Courses will correspond to those in a restaurant. A starter (soup, a fish course, or a special salad), the main dish, a green salad, cheeses, dessert or fruit.

- As the cheese board goes around at the end of the meal, cut yourself a share of the cheeses you want, maintaining the wedge shape. Take your share of the rind; don't take off the point. Watch how others cut the cheese, if you aren't sure.

- Peel and slice your fruit with your knife before eating it. (I eat the peel, usually, with apologies, as my Momma taught me the skin is the healthiest part.)

- An after dinner drink (*digestif*), either a sweet liqueur or a dry distilled product like Cognac, *eau-de-vie* or *marc*, will be offered. Now is the time to smoke, if you wish. Ask your host's permission, if no one else is smoking. Don't smoke between courses, unless others do.

- Write a thank-you note or call the next day to confirm the pleasure of the event.

THE PSYCHOLOGY OF CULTURAL ADJUSTMENT

As we already know from reading so far, coping with someone else's culture is stressful, but most essential for a successful multicultural life, especially if you are doing business. We cannot make the adjustments painless, but the more you understand the basic process, the better. For the professional and for the organisation that sent him or her abroad, cultural understanding and adjustments are required for success.

'La culture, c'est l'environment tangible et intangible édifié par l'homme^.' (Culture is that tangible and intangible environment man creates.)
—H Triandis

Culture shock is the beginning of cultural transition. It was described by P. Block in 1970 as 'primarily an emotional reaction that follows from not being able to understand, control and predict another's behaviour.'

Dr Kalervo Oberg, an anthropologist who defined the term 'culture shock' in 1960, says culture shock is brought on by 'the anxiety that results from losing familiar signs and symbols of social intercourse.'

Considered among the founding fathers in the field of cross-cultural communication, Oberg defined several aspects of culture shock for the United States Agency for International Development. To briefly summarise Oberg's findings, there are at least six aspects of culture shock:

- Strain due to the effort required to make necessary psychological adaptations.
- A sense of loss and feelings of deprivation in regard to friends, status, profession and possessions.
- Being rejected by and/or rejecting members of the new culture.
- Confusion in role, role expectation, values, feelings and self-identity.
- Surprise, anxiety and even disgust and indignation after becoming aware of culture differences.
- Feelings of impotence due to not being able to cope with the new environment.

THE STAGES OF CULTURE SHOCK

The pseudo-medical model of cross-cultural stress was developed first by Oberg and others and is still used today. Oberg's model is combined with the U-curve approach, developed about the same time, and described in detail in the book by Adrian Furnham and

Stephen Bochner, *Culture Shock: Psychological Reactions To Unfamiliar Environments.*

In the curve, the visitor starts with elation about the new culture, drops down into a trough of depression and confusion, then comes back up with a sense of satisfaction and optimism. This curve can happen many times, in varying intensity and over a varying period of time, but the cycle itself is now considered a normal reaction, though both mental and physical illness may be apparent. Using this model, we create a typical six-month cycle of attitudinal, emotional and physical responses you may have to France, or any other country which you visit for an extended period of time.

Pre-Departure
'I'm so excited! Paris, here I come.'

Activities	Planning, packing, processing, partying and parting.
Attitudes	Anticipation of new and interesting things. Lessening interest in current responsibilities.
Emotions	Enthusiasms and excitement, mixed with concern for leaving friends, relatives and a familiar environment. Children are particularly apprehensive and uncomfortable.
Physical response	Adults and children running on nervous energy. Difficulty sleeping.

The First Month
'Isn't it wonderful? Even more beautiful than the pictures.'

Activities	Welcoming and introductions. New foods, sights, sounds and people. Start learning the language, realising it is necessary.
Attitudes	Curiosity about the culture and the various opportunities. Downplaying the negative comments of other expatriates, the inability of waiters to understand you.

Emotions	Euphoria. You are really in France and it is really so beautiful.
Physical response	Some problems with all the food and wine, the condition known as *crise de foie*, a kind of hangover effect from too much rich butter, cream and fat in the diet. Some difficulty sleeping in a new place, with new night noises.

The Second Month
'This post office eats my letters.'

Activities	Moving into a permanent residence. Full job responsibilities and settling into a routine.
Attitudes	The charm of that tiny apartment and those exquisite menus of local restaurants start to pale. Growing awareness of what isn't available, or what is ridiculously expensive. Impatience with 'rude' waiters and 'indifferent' shopkeepers.
Emotions	Nervous, uncertain about how to function. Some withdrawal from the French, and seeking the familiar in friends and food.
Physical response	Colds and the flu (especially in winter). Gaining weight.

The Third Month
'I like France but I don't like the French.'

Activities	Language skills hit a plateau and seem to stop improving. People still don't understand you and work keeps you too busy to study, anyway. Work performance declines.
Attitudes	Discouraged, irritable, hypercritical. Negative cultural value judgements predominate. Conversations that

turn into long strings of complaints, stereotypical truisms seem to be confirmed.

Emotions	Depressed, discouraged and suspicious of strangers. Very lonely. Culture shock in extreme.
Physical response	Extreme fatigue, often illness.

The Fourth and Fifth Month

'You know, this is actually a very efficient way of doing it!'

Activities	Small victories in work and language study. Ways of getting things done are sorted out. Moments are competency bring hope. (If this does not begin to happen during this time, the visitor will usually give up).
Attitudes	Constructive and positive in outlook and potential. Accommodation to the French ways of doing things.
Emotions	Renewed interest in the country and in its people.
Physical response	Health restored.

The Sixth Month

'Your first visit? Well, don't miss...'

Activities	Routine established and visits now planned into other parts of the country with visiting friends. Local friendships established.
Attitudes	Maintain basic constructive attitude despite good days and bad days. Plateau reached.
Emotions	The ups and downs of life now accepted as normal, and a growing interest in helping others and reaching out to those who are struggling.
Physical response	Normal

Many aspects of individual personality and experience profoundly affect this basic formula. Your 'cycle' may be quite different, but few people will be able to learn much about their new culture without experiencing troughs of negative feelings and discouragement. Cultural stress can have profound negative effects on people, but it need not be treated as a disease.

S Bochner has developed a culture-learning model to deal with culture shock that looks for solutions by learning cultural characteristics that apply. Appropriate cultural skills are survival skills, in a way. Without them, the international attracts attention to himself as an outsider. Proper awareness, preparation and attitude can help the international accumulate these skills.

IS IT REALLY POSSIBLE TO BE MULTICULTURAL?

Yes! More and more work is being done in the field of multicultural life. Marriages, children, work and retirement are increasingly multicultural. There is a common comparison between learning a culture and learning a language, with as many stages of 'fluency' along the way. Multicultural expertise takes practice, but people can speak and act in more ways than one. They eventually do it subconsciously.

The biggest pitfall to multicultural understanding is assuming that cultural differences don't matter. The mediums of TV and cinema can change dress codes and language in an instant, but real cultural values change remarkably slowly. Businesses within the European Union are far more aware of this now than they were five years ago.

The ability to fly about the planet quickly and cheaply does not diminish the cultural differences into which we debark. It is much easier to get there, but it still takes time and effort to become culturally functional and years to feel truly 'at home'. But a multicultural life is hugely, wonderfully possible. We are all cultural chameleons, eager to 'fit in' wherever we are.

How to Develop Cultural Awareness

Furnham and Bochner describe several training techniques for developing social skills, and thus minimising culture shock:

- **Information-giving**

  This book is all about that and many more sources follow in the Further Reading section on page 244.

- **Cultural sensitisation**

  Real adaptation comes from observation, but there are ways you can fine-tune your observational skills. The first step is recognising that invisible difference between you and another person: cultural perspective. The Bloom Program, a course offered each October by the Women of American Church in Paris, integrates cultural sensitisation with basics on dealing with Paris. Details are available from the American Church and WICE.

  - Understanding the reason behind actions or attributes of another culture.

    One of my chief inspirations in the initial research for this book was a book called, in English, *Cultural Misunderstandings* by French anthropologist Raymonde Carroll. Her wisdom is scattered throughout this book and helped me enormously in understanding why the French do what they do, such as things they themselves often cannot describe. While few of us can aspire to be the talented social scientist Dr. Carroll is, I'd like to quote her five steps for developing cultural understanding:

  - Clear the deck.

    Avoid all attempts at discovering the deep-seated reasons for the cultural specificity of such-and-such a group. Although psychology, geography, history, religion and economics may be part of what people 'really are', these do not deal with the culture. Just seek to understand the culture, the system of communication.

- Be on the lookout.
  Listen to your own discourse, making judgements about people, 'The French are...' No. ' I find the French to be like this or that...' Yes, What is true is: another culture does not have the same characteristics as yours. Try to avoid judging these differences as good or bad.

- Recognise a 'cultural test' which is a sense of strangeness and unpleasantness, opacity in a certain situation. Remember the situation in as much detail as possible, before judgement has given it a broad stroke. Listen and watch with complete attention.

- Then analyse the experience to find an interpretation that can be verified elsewhere in the culture.

- Finally see, from this analysis, how other aspects of the culture might apply.

- Learning informally from 'old-hands' on site is another suggestion of Furnham and Bochner. It's informal and some information from 'older hands' is better than others, but it always helps to discuss your observations with others familiar with your problem.

- Formal Social Skills Training aimed at cross-cultural competence. This you will find in the section 'Professional Help in Cultural Understanding', on the next page.

PROFESSIONAL HELP IN
CULTURAL UNDERSTANDING

In addition to the many aspects of cultural differences and cultural awareness considered in this book, there are formal psychological and linguistic approaches now being developed to these 'invisible realities'. Both before your departure and after you arrive in France, you will find experts in the multi-disciplined field of cultural transition which may be of great help.

Choosing an Intercultural Trainer

If you are planning to do business in France or coming to live in France for any length of time, it would be well worth your while to get some intercultural training.

Kohls, again, offers some basic guidelines for choosing an international trainer who, he says, should have all the following qualifications:

- Personal knowledge of France and at least two years of living experience there.
- A positive attitude towards France and French people.
- The experience of having lived through culture shock, somewhere.
- A fundamental knowledge of the basic values of your home culture.
- Experience with stand-up training and experiential learning techniques.
- Interest in both content and process training.
- An image that is acceptable to the people being trained.

L Robert Kohls identifies four formal approaches to cross-cultural preparedness: education, which provides broad content knowledge of the subject country; training, which focuses on performing specific skills or meeting specific objectives effectively; orientation, which prepares a person to understand and function in another culture; and briefing, which provides a broad overview of a culture.

Aspects of numbers the first, third and fourth points are included elsewhere in this book and refer you to a number of resources, all included in the Bibliography. Many people are practising the second point), cross-cultural training. To find them contact:

Society For International Educational Training
and Research (SIETAR)
733 15th St. NW, Suite 900
Washington DC 20005 USA
Tel: (202) 296-4710
www.sietar.org

They have a scholarly journal, a newsletter, a listing of intercultural training specialists and networking services to other books and organisations.

GOING HOME... IT IS HARDER THAN YOU THINK.

Experienced cross-culturalists will tell you that the hardest part of the international experience is usually the return home. Though you never can totally integrate into another culture and you may not have even enjoyed the effort of trying, you will almost certainly find re-integrating into your first culture a difficult transition.

We adapt to other cultures in both conscious and subconscious ways. Re-adapting to our former cultural 'norms' takes a surprising amount of conscious effort. The changes we have made to adjust to something different are not instantly reversible, like switching languages.

Even if you conscientiously resist another culture, you pick up new habits in spite of yourself. We human beings can't help being conformists, and in the case of France, the temptation to conform to French ways is subtle and seductive.

Going home is another complex cultural transition, a new 'you' in an old cultural setting. It can take up to a year to adjust back. I have met many people doing business internationally who find going home the most difficult transition of all. They call it a kind of reverse homesickness.

The closer the culture is to your own, the more likely you are to be caught unawares. France, for another Westerner, ought to be an easy adjustment but it isn't. Going home ought to be easiest of all. Surprise! It is the hardest. When you examine them, the problems of going home are obvious. You are out of touch with local news and gossip. Yet it isn't so interesting now, in your new context.

Subconscious Adaptation

My favourite example of how unconsciously we learn to follow different rules in different cultures happened many years ago. A large group of Chinese businessmen were queued up properly with me at Heathrow Airport for one of the first non-stop flights to Hong Kong. I was impressed by their 'Britishness', waiting in line as we boarded the plane in a very orderly way. But when we landed at Hong Kong's Kai Tak Airport eight hours later, the wheels had hardly touched the tarmac before this same group were jumping up, grabbing their luggage from the overhead bins, and heading for the exit. While the cabin attendants managed to get them seated safely again for the taxi into the terminal, you can bet I was knocked aside when that seat belt sign went off and the door finally opened.

Your old friends cannot imagine or recognise the changes you have made. They are expecting the old you, with the shared old values and habits of home. They will be quickly bored by tales of your life abroad, even though they will express interest. Their lives revolve around a different centre and that is the centre they still share with you.

Your descriptions of life in France will soon be judged as 'bragging'. Don't wax poetic about the fancy French cuisine you've come to love while eating the hamburgers your friends have prepared for your welcome home party. You have seen enough of your friends' vacation photos and home movies to know how well yours will go over with them. A little goes along way. Likewise, any complaints you have about how difficult things were abroad will be taken lightly.

You have changed, in ways you didn't even know. This will intimidate everyone, even you. Just give yourself and your friends the patience and understanding you have learned to use abroad with strangers. You have another cultural adjustment to make, and it takes patience and conscious effort.

SETTLING IN

CHAPTER 5

'In North America stores are an extension of the
public space... communication in North American stores
is purpose driven. No one speaks to you except to help you
find what you need. But that's not the way in works
in France. The French store is considered the extension
of the owner's home—in many cases, it actually is.'
—*Sixty Million Frenchmen Can't Be Wrong*

YOU WILL NEED TO ARRIVE IN FRANCE PREPARED for bureaucracy. Be sure to bring with you: your driver's license, your marriage certificate, your birth certificate, any advanced educational or professional degree certificates you've earned, your international student ID card... all of these originals, as well as copies. Also, lots of copies of your passport photo, copies of all your bank accounts at home, your credit card numbers, and copies of receipts of all your major purchases which you are bringing with you, including home computers, stereo systems and other electronics.

There is a great book you should read before you move to France. Called *At Home in Paris*, it is written by the Junior Service League of Paris and partly sponsored by Disney Europe, whose American employees no doubt found it very useful. It covers hundreds of details of getting on in France. (*See* Further Reading *on page 244.*)

Also, of course, search the Internet! Just pay close attention to the sources of the information, to be sure you get reliable information. Print it out and bring it with you. Getting Internet access once in France can be complicated.

The Police

While you are living in a democracy in France, some different rules apply. For one thing, the national police (who also manage Paris) have the right to arrest and detain you as they deem proper. (Yes, Georgia, even if you are an American!) Never argue with a policeman unless you want a night in jail. I would not bother to ask them directions, either. Tourist assistance is not part of their job description.

Guilty Until Proven Innocent

As in many democracies, the tax authorities can deem you guilty until proven innocent when it comes to paying taxes. In my own case, I was sent a written notice while abroad in Hong Kong that my small *chambre de bonne* (maid's room) in Paris would be emptied of its furniture in order to pay back taxes I owed in a small village in France which I had never even visited.

Friends in France rallied for me and called the office involved, finally discovering that another woman with two of my names was the offending party. I had to write a letter and send a copy of my passport to prove I was not the same 'Sally Taylor' they were looking for!

In another case, an American friend in Paris accepted the mail of a colleague who had recently left the country. *Lettres Recommandées* began arriving for the friend from the tax office in the town where he had lived. The friend said to ignore them. Then one day my friend returned to his flat to find a notice on the door that HIS furniture would be removed to cover back taxes if they weren't paid up in 48 hours.

He called the tax office involved and tried to explain that the man they wanted had left the country. No luck. Again, he had to prove he was not the man they wanted!

VISAS AND WORK PERMITS

If you plan to stay in France for any period over three months, either as a student or as a worker, and your home country is not a member of the European Union, you must organise your visa in advance with the French Embassy or Consulate nearest to you. Your first visit is to pick up the forms, the list of documents to be filed and the list of medical doctors accredited by the French Consulate. Then, when all your documents are filled in and the medical examination complete, you must go back to the Consulate to file the formal request, with all your justifications in hand. It can take up to three months to get your visa.

The length of time it takes really depends on the kind of visa you need. The French Government has an excellent website, in English, describing in detail all the different combinations of visas and their requirements. Visit www.diplomatie.gouv.fr/venir/visas/index.asp?anglais.

Or google 'France visa' for loads of independent services to help you.

RENTING A PLACE

If your first task is finding a place to live in France, you have your work cut out for you. Pressure for flats in the City of Light is intense. Rents are high and spaces are small. A standard *deux-pièces* is normal for a couple... that's two rooms, not two bedrooms + living room + dining room. Kitchens and bathrooms do not count as rooms, for good reason—they are usually very small. Modern conveniences such as washing machines, dishwashers and microwaves may well be considered chargeable extras.

Buying Property

Very few restrictions remain for foreigners buying French real estate. (Farm land and protected cultural property are the exception.) Deeds must be prepared by special lawyers called *notaires*, though any lawyer can advise you on real estate law.

Taxes for the registration of the deed and expenses related to the purchase of the property, are paid by the buyer. Apart from the fees paid to the real estate agent (which are calculated from the sales price), you must expect to pay an extra 10 per cent of the property price if the property is to be used as a habitation and 20 per cent if the property is to be used professionally. This is the estimate of the registration taxes and expenses previously mentioned.

However, there are some considerations to be made when putting such property into your will. An excellent book by Vivienne Menkes-Ivry, *Buying A Home in France*, describes all the details. In another called *Living in France* by the Association of American Wives of Europeans, the legal aspects of wills are detailed.

When it comes to hunting for a place, you would be better off connecting with the foreign community, the American or English churches, for example. There are billboards at these organisations offering sublets and second-hand furniture by others leaving town. Also check the English language publications and ask their staff. Use the Internet first and contact the addresses in the Resource Guide on page 227.

RENTAL LAWS AND TENANTS' RIGHTS

Apart from commercial rental contracts, which are handled differently, the basic regulations for housing contracts apply, whether or not you are a French citizen. In some cases, you may sign a one-year lease, but the standard length is either three or six years. The tenant must give three months' notice of quitting; the owner, six months.

Commonly, the owner will ask for some guarantees (proof of revenues, a guarantee from a relative, etc.). A two-month rental deposit is normal. More is illegal. Fees and expenses of a real estate agency must be split equally between tenant and landlord.

It is very important that a thorough, written appraisal of the apartment or house be done before you sign the lease and before your departure, so that the owner cannot claim damages and keep your deposit. This is called a 'contradictory'. Both parties or their representatives must be present to sign.

You must ask for closing bills from the EGF (Electricité et Gaz de France) and France Telecom and pay them, before leaving. The landlord has the right to hold the deposit until you can prove you have paid all the bills.

You must insure your own belongings as well as the apartment or house against fire, water damage, etc. You are also liable for taxes related to the apartment. A tax of 2.5 per cent of the rent must be paid monthly. A flat *taxe d'habitation* must be paid by the tenant who inhabits the apartment as of 1 January each year. That amount depends on the size and location of the building.

Choosing a Flat

Some important things to consider:

- Neighbourhood. The range of characteristics is wide in Paris, including some pretty dangerous spots at night up in the north of the city (the 18th and 19th *arrondissements*) where drugs are a problem. But even here you will find very nice areas. Rather than hunt all over town, stick with a couple of neighbourhoods you like, walk through them to spot *louer* signs in windows, or at the small agences which usually both sell and rent apartments. Learn street names so you can recognise them in advertisements in weekly advertising sheets like *Particulier à Particulier*.

- *Quel étage?* The higher up the apartment, the more light and air you will have. If there is an elevator in the building, the flats high up will be expensive. If not, they will get cheaper as you go up. In older buildings, the most elegant apartments are on the lower floors. They will have high ceilings, tall windows and fancy interior details. Don't be put off by something on the fifth floor without an elevator, however, unless you have serious physical disabilities. You really do get used to climbing stairs and that extra bit of exercise will help your body compensate for the rich French meals to come.

- Noise. Paris streets are noisy. And the main roads through tiny little villages have trucks (lorries) thundering through all night. Consider your tolerance for this. (I have learned to consider the sound of sirens a lullaby.) Most French apartments have window shutters that close out noise, but they also close out light and air. Apartments opening onto courtyards, away from the street, are usually more expensive because they are quiet. If there are many apartments facing the courtyard or many people using the courtyard as an access, then voices and footfall can also be bothersome, too. Noise ricochets up those high stone walls.

- Concierges. If possible, get into a building with the old-style French concierge or *guardienne* (who will probably be Portuguese). These lovely women guard against nuisances like overflowing garbage, give personal attention to mail delivery and special notices, show in servicemen and they will hold an extra set of keys to your place, in case you lose yours. They are a delicious spice to your life, keeping you up with gossip, with politics and with protocol. Invaluable to the newcomer.

- Mail services. If your building hasn't got a concierge, your mailbox will be lined up inside the doorway. Make sure yours is locked. Often they are not big enough for magazines and your subscriptions will be left in a common trough, where they might disappear. Mail tampering is a problem in Paris, so arrange for a locking mailbox big enough for all your mail.

- Charges. You will have to pay two months' rent in advance, usually, as well as a fee to the agent. Make sure you get all the papers stating what you've paid and what you are due back at the end. (*See the section on* 'Rental Laws and Tenant's Rights' *on page 97 for your legal rights as a tenant in France.*)

- Red tape. France is built on a mountain of bureaucracy. It works, and some of it is quite sensible. But speed is not the primary consideration. As with everything in France, be patient. Finding an apartment and renting it takes time and good connections. (*see the 'System D' in* Chapter 3: Stereoptypes and Beyond—The Public French *on page 35*)

MAKING YOUR HOME AMONG THE FRENCH

Here are some tips on how to be a good neighbour, as well as how to keep up with Les Duponts (the Joneses).

A good relationship with the *gardienne*, if you are lucky enough to have one, makes life infinitely easier in France. A friendly manner and thoughtful remuneration for any special attention you get, as well as Christmas and Easter bonuses will help build your relationship. (Christmas should include cash, anywhere from 50 to 500 euros, depending on your rent and the number of special services she supplies).

The concierge will often be a good source for other service people you need: plumbers, electricians, carpenters. She usually knows who has done good work in the past in the building. She will also have good neighbourhood shopping tips.

The people she cannot help you with are your neighbours. Remember what you have already learned about the burdens of friendship. The French must maintain a careful distance with their neighbours. You are living at very close quarters to these other people in the building, squeezed into tiny elevators and commingling garbage. Yet you cannot possibly all become friends in the French sense.

The French, reasonably, maintain a certain respectful distance from their neighbours. (Let them show you how.) You always make a polite acknowledgement of their presence, when you meet in the hallway, stairwell or elevator, but a respectful silence beyond that. The coolness allows both of you your privacy. It is not a 'put down' or rude. It is polite.

You also provide certain considerations. Hold the door for anyone coming in behind you (as most people do, even in the *métro* stations in France). Avoid making unnecessary noise in the public areas of the building, as well as in your own quarters. In old stone buildings, noise travels. Consider the effect of your footfall and chair scraping on the neighbours below. You will be expected to behave in a way that assures everyone else their comfort and quiet.

Sooner or later, you will begin to make better friends among your neighbours. No friend is a better and more loyal one than a French person, but like all good things, they need time. Even in the countryside, you will find people hesitant to step forward, at first. Speak French and be patient. Remember the French love to be amused and you are probably a fairly capable person at doing so.

MANAGING AT HOME IN FRANCE

If you are coming to work in France, be sensitive to the peculiar set of problems of your partner and children. The person in the family whose job brings them here is lucky. He has a specific assignment in his own field of endeavour and a workplace. These bridge some of the deepest troughs of cultural divide. Unemployed spouses and children must go about all of their normal activities in totally new ways. They have many more culture adjustments to make and few guides for making them.

In most multinational companies, one out of three employees sent abroad comes home early. Robert Kohls says studies show four out of five early returns because the spouse, not the employee, couldn't adjust.

Here are some of the complaints I heard from housewives abroad: "My husband's company said we could bring whatever we wanted with us, so I brought everything, right down to soap and toilet paper. Although he said it was silly, that such things would be available here in France, I knew it might be difficult to find the things I wanted. For example, I forgot shampoo and spent two hours and $20 finding what I hoped was equivalent to what we use at home. My husband was furious."

"As a wife here, the very things which I did at home with expertise are suddenly a whole new ball game. I have to reinvent the wheel. None of my expertise in shopping and keeping house in America applies here."

"Why didn't anyone tell us it was going to be so hard?" complains another spouse. "I came to Paris expecting

Battling Loneliness

You may experience bouts of loneliness, especially in the middle of Paris. Try some of these...

- Go to the movies. All movie houses discount their prices on Mondays. Read *Pariscope* or *L'Officiel* for the details. If your French isn't great, go to the English or American ones showing in version original. (VO)
- Ask your friends to come visit (few will need to be asked twice) and look up friends-of-friends, who are often glad to meet another foreigner.
- Join English-speaking organisations, as suggested in the appendix of this book. They offer activities that will teach you more about France and the French.
- Get yourself established as a 'regular' in one of the neighbourhood restaurants. They will make you feel welcomed when you are eating alone. They will even set you up with other interesting 'singles' so you can have an interesting conversation as you dine together. (*see* Chapter 6: Restaurants and Wine—The French Essentials *on page 120*.)

a wonderful, romantic experience, and I feel lost and alone. It's much harder to find work, to find apartments, than I expected. My husband has no sympathy with my problems. I feel like an innocent victim and it makes me angry."

Books such as this one, and organisations like Women In Continuing Education (WICE) help. But there are many details to manage. Be patient and help as much as you can.

CHILDREN AND THEIR ADJUSTMENTS

Children are naturally more culturally adaptable than adults, but when you first put them into a strange, new setting, they are going to look to you as the model for their adjustment attitudes. A positive approach to your new life in France, taking it all as a new family adventure, will greatly help your children adjust.

Clinical psychologist Paul Marcille, who works with family adjustment problems in Paris, says that children mirror their parents' attitude. Pushing kids to adapt to their new surrounds on their own won't work. You have to stick together.

A child's needs will depend on his developmental stage in life. A very young child will be more concerned about losing his favourite TV programmes, than his friends in day care. He is still learning his first culture, mostly by observation and repeating what you do, so he can continue the same approach with the new culture.

An adolescent, who is normally trying to establish his independence from parents and family, will miss his peer group and will probably need your support more than he is able to admit. Your sensitivity can improve your child's adjustment skills now and for the rest of his life. Children rarely have negative reactions to a new environment unless their parents teach them by their own example. It has also been proven that children who learn multicultural skills early in life have a distinct advantage as adults in international settings.

Recognise the potential problems early, and seek professional help if you don't feel you can handle them.

For helpful sources, please refer to the Resource Guide on page 227.

EDUCATION IN FRANCE

As a resident paying French taxes, you can take advantage of the French educational system. If you have very young children, you are in luck! The French government offers *école maternelle* for children from the age of two until five, when they enter kindergarten for a year, then the first grade. Although these schools stop for lunch and close on Wednesdays, there are *cantines* and *garderies* to fill in the gaps for working mothers.

Don't worry about the language differences with your very young. Children below the age of nine pick up new languages as easily as their first one. Most international families who come to France quickly bow to their children's superior ability to communicate in French, even if the whole family started at the same skills level.

The French Government offers child care to all from the age of two.

Once a child reaches the age of nine, however, he starts to learn languages more slowly. If you have such school-age children who do not have French language skills when they come, you might consider an English-speaking school for the first year, and moving on to a bilingual school after that.

There are a number of French bilingual schools (called *bilingues*) which you might well consider as an alternative to expensive, private English-language education in France. These *bilingues* get high ratings among international students I've talked to. One bright young international lady I know contrasts the pretence of friendship she has found at her English-language school with the more honest, but cooler reception from classmates at the *bilingue* school. Isolating English speakers from the French community gives children a harmful sense of superiority.

If your children are younger than nine or have strong French skills already and if you plan to stay in France until their education is complete, you should certainly consider a regular French school. They are very good, but very competitive, geared for that final Baccalaureat exam, which will dictate your child's future opportunities for study at the *Grandes Ecoles*.

Guide to Education

The Association of American Wives of Europeans has published an excellent *Guide to Education*, discussing in detail the whole subject of bilingual and monolingual education in France. It is available from the American Church in Paris or AAWE (*see the* Resource Guide *on page 227*).

In their booklet, they pose several important questions you should consider when choosing a bilingual school:

- What subjects are taught in English?
- Are English classes separated by ability or just age?
- What are the students' record for further education?
- What percentage of students are multicultural?

THE TELEPHONE

Twenty years ago, the French had one of the worst phone systems in the world, but as often happens in France, a group of French bureaucrats applied themselves to the problem and the French phone service leapt ahead of everyone, surprising even the French themselves. Bravo for strong centralised governments!

The phones in France work well, they are reasonably priced, and as in the rest of the planet, cell phones are now ubiquitous. They have outnumbered land lines since 1999.

If you aren't staying long in France, you can buy or bring your own programmable GSM (European standard) cell phone. Then buy a chip from any one of several French cell phone service suppliers including Orange and SFR. That will give you a French phone number which you can keep as long as you keep using the phone. You then buy debit cards with time value and enter those into your phone. Each cell phone chip supplier has his own debit card system. Their retail shops are everywhere and offer a wide range of telephones, gadgets and Internet services as well.

Dialing the Telephone

Every number in France and its DOM (overseas departments such as Guadeloupe) is now a ten-digit number. Each number starts with a '0', followed by one or several numbers that indicate the geographic location and then the local number. Thus you have to dial the full ten-digit number, whether you are calling from down the street or across the country or over from the Caribbean. You pay for the call at different rates, depending on the distance and time of day. Local calls are not free.

If you want to make calls outside of France or to the French overseas territories (TOM), you dial two zeros, then the country code and the rest of the number. If someone from home wants to call you in France, he dials his own international access code, the country code for France (33) then, dropping the first '0', he dials the remaining nine-digit number.

It is still relatively easy to use the public phone system in France, found in handsome glass boxes all over the country. Most now require the use of a card, either a debit or a credit card. The debit phone card, the 'Telecarte', is available everywhere, from street kiosks, metro stations, tobacco shops and post offices in a variety of values. Insert the card and the phone will automatically deduct the cost and display the dwindling value of your card as you talk. The speed at which the value declines depends on the distance of the call. Calls within France are quite reasonable. Should the card run out of value as you are talking, you can insert another card, if you have it handy, without losing the connection.

To subscribe to a land line telephone service, just drop into your neighbourhood France Telecom office. Land lines come with a free messaging service, so you don't need an additional answering machine.

In the 1980s, France Telecom jumped ahead of the Internet Revolution with their Minitel monitor plus keyboard hardware. This little electronic gem was offered free, or at minimal charge, to all French telephone subscribers. It changed the way the French communicated with each other and with the world, years before the Internet. The only bother is adjusting to their French keyboard, which switches around a few letters, just enough for them to drive a touch typist wild.

The time spent on the Minitel is tracked and billed by France Telecom. They have all sorts of services, from the national telephone directory to train reservation services direct with the train company. You can also find services that bring men and women together for notorious leisure time activities. Ah, only in France!

You reach the *annuaire* (national telephone directory) by dialing '3611' on the Minitel. (You can find a Minitel at most Post Offices if you don't have one at home.) To make train reservations, dial '3615' then punch in 'SNCF'. You can find the other services on your own.

The Minitel has been overshadowed now by personal computers and the Internet. But the French excel here, too. You can access the regional train services on www.

ratp.fr, the national trains at www.sncf.com and the TGV at www.tgv.com. Even the French yellow pages are online at: http://www.pagesjaunes.fr.

THE COLOUR OF MONEY

The French have a very uncomfortable relationship with money. They relish expressions of sensuality in nearly all its forms, yet they find the subject of money indecent. Socially, of course, 'old money' is more respectable than 'new money' and third generation nouveaux riches are distinguished from those coarser first generation nouveaux riches. But these are finer subtleties of social status.

'L'argent n'a pas d'odeur.'
(Money has no scent.)

Basically, making money is not admired, being rich and flaunting it is *gauche,* and the topic of money itself is not a favourite for discussion. It is very impolite to ask someone what he does to make money.

No French person wants to be judged on the basis of how he makes his living. This is quite difficult for Americans and Asians to understand. Even in business, no particular status is awarded to a person based on how much money he has or how quickly he has proven he can make it. In Hong Kong and New York, money is the measure of all things. In France, being wealthy is more likely to be held against you.

Much better to come to France as an author, professor or musician and be amusing and enlightening if you want quick social acceptance. If you are here to do business, you will find your French colleagues exhibiting this underlying ambivalence towards money from the start.

Cash For Travellers

While banking in France is very efficient, bank transfers between countries outside the European Union are still ridiculously slow and expensive. Travellers cheques cost both when you buy them and when you sell. It is best to use international credit and debit cards like Visa and Mastercard when you travel. They work in most cash machines around the world, using the same PIN number you use at home. Most credit card companies charge you for this service, but most banks honor the best rate of the day on the exchange. So it is worth it. Just don't lose your card. And be sure to keep a home number to call and report a lost card. Not an '800' number, as they usually don't work abroad.

OPENING A BANK ACCOUNT

Banking is done as discreetly as possible in France, to avoid everyone's embarrassment over dealing with m-o-n-e-y. French banks look more like second-class airline offices and French banking personnel dress down, some even wearing blue jeans. They are often seated comfortably behind their counters, almost out of view.

The Euro

France, as part of the European Union, replaced the Frenchfranc with the new unit of currency on 1 January 2002. The euro is available in eight coins (2 euro, 1 euro, 50 cent, 20 cent, 10 cent, 5 cent, 2 cent, and 1 cent) and seven bills (500 euro, 200 euro, 100 euro, 50 euro, 20 euro, 10 euro and 5 euro). Despite the remarkable success of the transition to the euro, a few of the French continue to speak of prices in terms of the former currency, the franc, especially in large sums. Thus, it is useful to know that 1 euro is worth approximately 6.56 French francs (fixed rate).

Most banks use an open-counter design, creating as casual a situation as possible between you and the person handling your money. There is a major security effort at the entrance, where you will often have to go through two doors, each opening only when the other is closed. If a bank robber comes in, they simply trap him between the doors as he leaves. Very efficient.

Shopping Hours

Taking into consideration the lunch hours (anytime from 12 noon to 3:00 pm), shops in the major cities open from 10:00 am till about 7:00 pm or 8:00 pm from Monday through to Saturday.

The post office is open from 8:00 am to 7:00 pm, Monday through to Friday. On Saturday, they open for half a day till 12 noon. Banks are usually open from 9:00 am to 4:30 pm, Monday through to Friday. They remain closed on Saturday. The stock exchange (Bourse) trades from 11:30 am to 2:30 pm, Monday through Friday. Some department stores also have a late night shopping day once a week, when they open till 9:00 pm. To cater to the working population, *hypermarchés* operate late till 9:00 pm or 10:00 pm from Monday through Saturday. Most establishments are closed on Sunday. Shops that stay open on Saturday or Sunday usually close Mondays. Don't panic, at least one *boulanger* or *pâtissier* in each neighbourhood will open both Sunday and Monday so the French and other *croissant* and *baguette* addicts can have their fresh 'hit' for the day. Just don't be surprised to find many restaurants and art galleries closed on Monday.

In the event of an emergency, after-hours services include:

- **Post Office**
  Open 24 hours at 52, rue du Louvre, 1er
  Tel: (01) 4233-7160. If taking the Métro, alight at Louvre.
- **Currency Exchange**
  Open everyday from 6:30 am to 11:00 pm at Gare de Lyon.

To open a French bank account, you must be 18 years old, have a valid piece of identity (passport or *carte de séjour*) and proof of residence (telephone bill or *Electricité et*

Although French people dislike talking about money, yet the LOTO, a lottery game, is popular among men and women of all ages over 18. Tickets are sold wherever the sign is displayed.

Gaz de France bill). Most banks offer both savings accounts and checking accounts. Even the regular post office offers banking services.

You will receive your cheques in a few days and your *carte bleue* (CB, the name used in France for any credit or debit card) in a couple of weeks. Most banks link your CB card to the bank account in a debit system, so when you pay with your CB, the amount is deducted automatically from your checking account the next month.

You can also use the CB card as a cash card at money machines all over France, using your PIN, or personal identity code number. Your foreign credit card will probably work, too.

Some bank accounts, especially at the post office, limit the number of withdrawals you can make in a week, and some machines charge for withdrawals. Some savings accounts, like the Postépargne, offer both cheque writing and cash cards.

Many people in France have their salaries deposited directly into their bank accounts and their monthly bills, like EGF, telephone, etc., are deducted automatically. Automatic deductions are postponed until you have had ample warning, by mail. They are an easy way to get your monthly money chores done.

It is a major *faux pas* and a serious crime to overdraw a checking account in France. Thus, French cheques are readily accepted everywhere, often without a piece of identification, making a French account a very convenient thing to have. As the *carte bleue* and other credit and debit cards become more popular, though, these are preferred. However, take care punching in your PIN number in public view. You don't want anyone to know your code.

HEALTH CARE AND SOCIAL SERVICES

There are three main branches of government services, as they relate to you and your family: health care, retirement and unemployment pensions and family allowances. Employers, employees and the state all contribute to pay for these services. Even if you are not a French citizen, if someone in your family is working in France and paying taxes, you have the right to use them.

Both public and private health care services are available. You pay directly for treatment and medicines, then you are reimbursed by the government if you are eligible. If you are not, you should not come to live in France without some kind of health insurance, preferably one that includes repatriation coverage, so you can return to your home country for extended care. You won't get a visa to live in France without your own health insurance.

The Women's Institute for Continuing Education (WICE) has a very complete book Health Care Resources in Paris, which is worth buying if you are going to be in France for any length of time. Copies are available at WICE.

French hospitals have a fairly relaxed pace. Doctors give patients ample stays and patients are expected to supply their own pyjamas, robes, towels and toiletries... even for their newborn babies! The price of both medical supplies and services are government controlled.

Medicines and medical supplies are sold at pharmacies displaying the green cross. The pharmacists have sufficient medical training to advise you on common medical problems. They can prescribe medicines, based on your symptoms. If they think you should see a doctor, they will recommend appropriate specialists in the neighbourhood, both private and public. Best of all, they are required by law to know their mushrooms. Take the ones you just found in the woods to them first to be sure they are edible!

Emergency medical care is Service d'Aide Médicale d'Urgence (SAMU) and the Paris number is 15. The number for English-speakers is operated by S.O.S. Médecins at 01.47.23.80.80. If your case is not life-threatening, but you are too sick to go to a doctor, there are on-call physicians who will come to your home 24 hours a day, 365 days a year, for a reasonable price, through S.O.S. Médecins. But look upon the local pharmacist as your first doctor's visit.

GETTING AROUND TOWN
French traffic is exhilarating—or terrifying—depending on your attachment to this existence and your understanding of French rules of the road, written and unwritten.

The French appear to have little concern for life or property once behind the wheel of an automobile. They take pride in their highly developed driving skills, which they believe is the reason that fewer tourists and Frenchmen die in road accidents each year. (In fact it is because the rules are finally being strictly enforced).

Up until 2002, France had the highest traffic fatality rate in Europe. Then President Chirac took up the challenge and by enforcing stricter traffic laws, he succeeded in reducing deaths by 20 per cent. Not that you should relax. The French highways still are still more dangerous than those of Britain (the safest in Europe), America or Germany.

TAXIS
Riding in a Paris taxi should be sufficient as a lesson to you. Like other French drivers, these men and women, strapped into their beautiful new Mercedes and Peugeots, can stop on a dime, roar to 100 kmph (62 mph) in seconds, and judge the perimeter of their vehicle to less than a centimetre.

Buckle your seatbelt. Consider yourself on a carnival ride and be grateful it's some other poor soul out there, and not you, trying to cross the street. You'll be among the hapless pedestrians soon enough.

Taxis are expensive in Paris. There are extra charges for time and mileage, which are indicated on the meter, a surcharge for bags put in the boot or trunk, for waiting and for evening services. Charges go up to the maximum just as the *Métro* stops at midnight. The tip expected is 5–10 per cent of the fare.

But you have at the wheel a *raconteur*, as well as a driver. Don't be afraid to engage in serious political discussion as the fellow negotiates seemingly impossible feats of traffic ballet.

PRIVATE TRANSPORTATION

When you begin walking around Paris (the very best way to enjoy it), keep those first performances in mind. Watch carefully at the crosswalks and DON'T jaywalk! If you really insist on driving, you will need an international driver's licence, plus your own country's driver's licence, and you must be 18 or older. Purchase insurance for your car, or pay for it when you rent one. Those centimetres can get very thin.

Top speed, officially, in Paris is 50 kmph (31 mph), 90 kmph (55.8 mph) on other roads and 130 kmph (80.6 mph) on the autoroutes. At intersections of equally important streets, not otherwise marked, the vehicle on the right ALWAYS has the right of way, except in a circle like the Arc de Triomphe, where the vehicles already circling take priority over those coming in. Red traffic lights get ignored regularly. When the light turns green in your favour, look before you charge out there.

As a driver, you really aren't supposed to hit anything or anybody in French traffic, though you can get very close. You want to be the guy in the superior position, especially if you don't have the right of way. One way to achieve that is simply by not making eye contact with the other car or driver. Ignoring him forces him to accommodate you. Once he notices that you have seen him, you have to give him his right of way.

The Parking Game

Parking has been elevated to an art form in Paris. There aren't enough places to park in Paris, even though most cars are quite small and there are many underground parking lots. The French consider this a challenge, a chance to demonstrate their creativity. It is something like a dance.

The first rule is: the rules were made to be broken. Improvisation is part of '*Le Système D*' for *Débrouiller*. You will learn the tricks in many bureaucratic elements of French life.

The second rule of the game is: the more clever the breach of the parking law, the better the status points for the driver.

You will see many creative parking jobs in Paris. Some have parking tickets already on them. Meter maids in Paris have backbones of steel. There is even a clever little two-seater French car just long enough to fit the width of the parking lane, very popular in Paris.

If you do something really wrong, you will be reprimanded. This can involve you in things like horn-blowing contests, shouting and fist-waving with other drivers and even pedestrians.

Fay Sharman says the French treat their cars the way they treat women. Though I am grateful that hasn't been my experience, I must admit I enjoy watching French traffic. From the relative safety of a Paris sidewalk cafe, you will find the confrontations, contortions and brilliant near misses highly amusing.

CYCLING

From the pedestrian's perspective, the cyclist in Paris is a lunatic. But when you are on the bicycle, you only see the beautiful city in front of you, never the mad, oncoming traffic jostling for position behind you. Happily, they always make room for you!

The Tow Truck That Could

One summer evening, I dined outside at a narrow, five-street intersection in an old and congested part of Paris. Two of the five streets came together at a sharp angle, forming a triangle of extra pavement after the sidewalk ended and before the streets actually merged. Several small cars were wedged illegally into that triangle, parked just inside the point, like the tip of a triangle of brie cheese.

Just after I sat down at my table, I saw a tow truck pull up. Now, French tow truck drivers express an art form of their own. Extricating tightly parked cars from extremely narrow streets is their speciality. Everyone at the restaurant watched as this fellow strapped, lifted, loaded and carted away the illegally parked car furthest out in the triangle. Not a single scratch. It was masterful. I applauded as he disappeared around the corner.

I had just given my order, when another car came along, assessed the opening and parked in that same spot. We diners watched silently. The driver got out and strutted away, quite pleased with his cleverness and ingenuity.

My first course had just arrived when the tow truck came back. Carefully plucking this latest parking violator from what was clearly his 'regular' space, his audience watched and applauded again. This little drama repeated all evening.

None of us attempted to break the cycle by stopping the parking violators. How could we? It would have meant standing guard in the street all evening instead of enjoying our meal. Anyway, each driver had such a look of accomplishment as he strutted away. And that tow truck driver never let us down. It was a modern Myth of Sisyphus, performed through the night and into eternity, no doubt, by a faithful corps of civil servants and the endlessly creative drivers of Paris. It certainly inspired me to stick to my preferred mode of private transportation in Paris, the bicycle.

Best of all, you can slip gracefully between lanes of clogged traffic, and meander along to your destination when everyone else is stopped in their tracks. In 1996, they began installing very helpful bicycle lanes in Paris, protected from motorists with high bumps and clearly marked. They are abused by madmen on motor scooters, the biggest threat to cyclists and motorists alike in Paris today. But a middle aged lady on a bike with high wide handlebars and her shopping strapped on the back makes a good deterrent.

Nearly everybody is nice to a cyclist in France and this is statistically affirmed. The high number of French traffic fatalities, includes a disproportionately small number (17 per cent) of pedestrians and bicyclists.

The bicycle was invented in France, and nearly every Frenchman follows the sport of bicycle racing, especially the Tour de France, which gives every follower a tour of the country, as well as marking the beginning of summer holidays.

But for those not devoted to *La Petite Reine* (the little queen) as she is known, the law also favours two-wheeled vehicles over four-wheeled vehicles in the courts. So, if an automobile hits a bicycle in France, he is apt to have to pay the damages, regardless of who was at fault.

For three decades of riding a bicycle in Paris traffic, no one has ever blown their horn, waved their fist or shouted at me. The French love their *petite reine* and they give her room. As a result, Paris traffic is manageable on a bicycle, at least to an alert and seasoned urban cyclist. I recommend it, though I wear a helmet (still not *á la mode* in Paris).

The countryside of France is nothing short of magnificent on a bicycle (that is another book.) The SNCF allows you to bring your bicycle on most suburban trains and to check it into baggage when you are travelling longer distances. They also rent bicycles at most of the major train stations.

PUBLIC TRANSPORTATION

The French philosophy of *égalité* really shines here. *Le Métro* is the oldest underground public transportation system in the world, and it is linked up with all the rest of the public transportation system, including the newest, fastest trains in the world, the TGV. You can go everywhere in the country conveniently by some sort of public conveyance, especially if you begin and end in Paris.

People are generally polite in public transport. They will hold the door for the person behind them. They will let people exit a train or bus before getting on. They will relinquish a seat for the elderly or the handicapped. You should remember to do the same.

All classes of people use the *métro* and the buses of Paris, so addresses often note the nearest *métro* station with an 'M', and the name of the station. The city system uses little green cardboard tickets you buy in the *métro* stations (cheaper by the ten-pack or *carnet*). You can get a monthly pass, as well. These also work on the buses. Children under ten ride at half price. A first class car in the middle of some trains is reserved for first-class ticket buyers from 9:00 am to 5:00 pm but open to everyone the rest of the time.

Since 'no smoking' rules were instituted in the underground, they are cleaner and more pleasant. I just don't like being underground. If I can't cycle (due to major rain or snow) I prefer to ride the buses and see the city. The *métro* is definitely faster, especially at rush hour.

Look at the maps posted on the handsome glass bus stops and in the *métro* to figure out your route. There is one map for each system. You should have your own maps, too. Even the French look at these maps, though they try to do so fleetingly.

On the buses you must *composter* your ticket by pushing it into a red slot that loudly punches it as 'used'. Buses are boarded at the front and exited in the middle. (Say '*Bonjour, Monsieur*' to the driver.)

From the sleek TGV to the centenarian Metro system, everyone uses public transportation in France.

Many bus services stop at 8:00 pm (the maps explain which ones). Most buses and all *métro* services stop by 1:00 am and don't start again until 5:30 am. Taxis accommodate by raising their prices to the maximum during these hours.

Trains in France are generally clean, fast and inexpensive. The TGV (*Trains à Grande Vitesse*) reaches a maximum speed of 300 kmph (186 mph) and zips from Paris (Gare de Lyon) to Marseilles in four hours, as well as many other destinations. The Eurostar goes from Paris (Gare du Nord) to London in three hours, under the English channel. You need reservations for these trains, however, and as different ones start from different stations in Paris, be sure you get to the right station. (Remember the star pattern!)

RESTAURANTS AND WINE— FRENCH ESSENTIALS

CHAPTER 6

MADAM MIGHT PREFER THE TURBOT...
BUT THERE AGAIN, MAYBE THE...

MENU

TRIGG.

'Paris is the only city I know where you have
an absolute desire to go out into the streets,
to walk or to drop into a café.'
—William Gardner Smith

LE CAFÉ—EVERYDAY FARE IN PARIS

The café in France is something comparable to the dim sum teahouse tradition of China, except smokier. Sitting for hours in the teahouse, talking and eating dim sum would seem very familiar to the Frenchman, who loves nothing better than sitting, alone or with friends, in a café, or whenever weather permits, outdoors on the sidewalk.

With his little cup of express and his cigarette, he can observe the world and, in conversation among friends, he can describe just how it needs changing. (If you can't tolerate cigarette smoke, be sure to sit outside, or by the door. Many places have *non-fumeur* sections now, but ventilation is sometimes poor.)

Café, Thé, or

The French normally drink their coffee in little cups, very strongly brewed and black. This can be browned with a little milk and called a *noisette*, or doubled by adding an equal amount of hot milk and called a *crème*. It can also be watered down and served in a large cup as an *allongé*. If these powerful little brews are too much for you, try a *citron pressé*, freshly squeezed lemon juice to which you add sugar and water to suit your taste, or any number of non-alcoholic *sirops*, flavoured concentrates (already sugared) you dilute with water. Otherwise. try the lovely herbal teas called *infusions* that come in many different beneficial flavours.

It only takes a little bit of sunshine to get the French out onto the sidewalk for their café or drinks.

Talking philosophy and politics and watching the world go by (both the pedestrians and the traffic) are the two favourite pastimes in France. The relaxed atmosphere of a French café can dispel the chill of loneliness far better than TV can.

The French still make a distinction between the joy of accumulation and the accumulation of joys. I can sit for hours at a sidewalk café, with a book or postcards to write, watching the French enjoy a sunny afternoon. For rainy days, I go snuggle up inside with a *Pariscope* and plan my next cultural activity. The total cost is a single purchase of coffee: about 2 euros. No respectable café owner would consider disturbing the long, peaceful perusals of a client, even one who just buys a single express.

Since the turn of the century, the café has been an important part of social life in France. For many with small dinghy apartments, it is a home away from home. You will find the patron quite hospitable, except during the busy lunch hours. At other times, he will often engage you in conversation, once he is confident you share a common language.

Variations on the Café

There are several varieties on the café theme in France. They each work slightly differently, so here's a general rundown:

- **La brasserie** will be similar to a café, but larger or smarter, with a dining area featuring a wider selection of food, usually served all day. This is where to go if you are hungry at 6:00 pm! The same stay as-long-as-you-like rule applies, but if you sit in the dining area, you will be expected to order a hot meal.

- **Le bar** in France is usually much smaller than a café. You pop inside for a quick drink and often stand for service. Excellent for a quick express and vocal political discussions but not for long, intellectual conversations. The clientele is mostly older men of working class and the conversation will usually revolve around French sports. Perfect, if you are a soccer fan.

- **Le bar à vin.** The atmosphere here is more along the lines of a café, but with wines from a specific region featured by the glass or the bottle. The food will also be regional—plates of meats (*charcuterie*) and cheeses with fine bread to complement the wines. Here the interest in the wines creates a particularly friendly ambience in the best café tradition. A wine bar is also an excellent place to learn more about the nuances of the many wines regions of France. The employees will all be enthusiasts. (*See* Chapter 7: The Greatest Arts of France *on page 141*.)

- **Le salon de thé** is a more feminine, upmarket version of the café. Sweet pastries and little *canapés* will be made and sold, usually to take away for some elegant event at home, for tea or for dessert at a fine dinner. There will be a few tables where you can eat these specialities in the shop, served along with tea, an *infusion* or coffee or even an alcoholic beverage. Service usually runs all day and some expand the menu at lunch time. Conversation is rather more discreet, delivered at a lower volume. There will be no bar and little camaraderie. I always imagine couples at a *salon de thé* to be clandestine lovers.

- **Fast food places** now abound in France, wherever students or tourists congregate. Just like at home, they are brightly lit, loud and impersonal, with lousy food. I avoid them.

He might pull in his 'regulars' lined up at *le zinc*, the bar, where drinks are cheaper. You will soon begin to feel at home, too. (*See* Chapter 4: Fitting into the French Way of Life *on on 45 to find out how to get started turning the French into friends.*) If you are alone, you will sometimes get better, if not faster, service and you will be more quickly incorporated into the conversation at the bar. It is a great idea to pick a café or little restaurant in your neighbourhood that you like and visit regularly. You will soon feel like part of the family.

A Café Lunch

Lunch time in Paris is fun, if a bit challenging. Just don't expect 'fast food' service, even in a café. In the heat of things, waiters will speak quickly, often too busy to find you a menu (the day's specials will be written on a chalkboard). You might have to wait for *l'addition* (the bill).

To get that bill, just catch your waiter's eye and discreetly pretend you are writing on your palm. If you really want his attention, never call out "*Garçon!*" Say politely, "*Si'l vous plaît*" and raise your hand slightly as you catch his eye.

French cafés serve simple hot lunches during the business week and every table will be taken. This noontime respite used to take two hours, though most Parisians are in more of a hurry now.

The food menu will not be lengthy: *un plat varié* of vegetables in season with a piece of ham, an *entrecôte* steak with *pommes frites*, a couple of *salades* and one or two tarts for dessert. Get a glass of wine (*read more about wine on page 131*) and a *carafe d'eau,* a pitcher of water, which is free. Outside of lunch time, mainly sandwiches or hot *croque-monsieurs* will be available, along with salad, ice cream and any tarts left over from lunch time.

You'll find exceptions to this generally friendly scene, of course, especially where cafés cater to mobs of tourists taking a brief pause between the tourist spots. Near the Opéra and American Express, along the Champs Elysée (now mostly fast food places anyway), and around the Louvre, sidewalk cafés have taken on the ambience of their non-Parisian clientele.

Tourists unsure of themselves sit stunned or exhausted while others oblivious of their surroundings talk loudly to their friends in languages other than French, usually about things 'back home'. This 'culture shocked' scene I try to avoid.

If you want to practise your French, sit at the bar (*le zinc*, from the days when they were covered with that) with a glass of wine or a beer (*un demi* is plenty). The regulars will happily indulge their curiosity about you. All drinks will be a bit cheaper here than at a table. If you later move to a table, the price of what you already bought will go up, automatically. You will be expected to pay for all you've consumed only when you leave, though the waiter may leave a little slip of paper under your plate to keep track of your addition as you go along.

Children are welcome and can even be served alcohol legally as long as they are at least 14 years of age.

WHY BUSINESSES CLOSE FOR LUNCH

Following the sage advice of Richelieu in the 17th century, the most hyperactive Frenchman still spends a good chunk of his day sitting leisurely *à table*. The enjoyment of food and wine pervades all classes in France, and those two hours for the midday meals are still held sacred in most parts of France.

In a Small Village

You are really lucky if you arrive in a small village at lunch-time, deep in the French countryside. Nearly everything will be shuttered, but don't worry. Circle the main square and usually near the church you will find one or two little restaurants serving glorious country cuisine in generous quantities, family-style, with endless carafes of local wine. Not *haute cuisine* but life doesn't get much better..

In Paris and the other major cities, international business standards have shortened *le dejeuner* to a mere one hour (though people linger) and the four-course meal with wines to two courses with *eau minérale*.

Fortunately, there is not much else you can do in most of France from 12:30–2:30 pm. Most shops and banks close as everyone flocks to the cafés and restaurants. In more traditional families, where employment still allows the luxury, the midday meal will be served at home. Children even come home from school.

Surviving Lunch

Warning! To indulge in a three- or four-course meal with wine at lunch-time spells functional disaster for the remainder of the day. Don't ask me how the French do it. Following a tiny breakfast of *un express* and *croissant*, they eat luxuriously at lunch and/or dinner, yet still appear clear headed. And they always keep trim. I need a nap after a typical French midday meal. And I won't even start comparing figures. But it's worth it.

REFINED DINING AND THE FOOD MYSTIQUE

A lovely, almost holiday mood persists in good French restaurants at lunch-time, with great conversation and special dishes. A professional restaurateur treats you as a discriminating guest and encourages you to linger, to feel 'at home'. This is your table for today.

Service is purposely slow, allowing you to settle in, talk to your friends, choose your dishes and enjoy each part of your meal. Hurrying creates indigestion, as your mother certainly told you. Take a table outside and enjoy one of the great pleasures of being alive and in France.

How to Order a Fine Meal

Your best value is usually *le menu* or the *prix fixe*. This set meal at a set price usually offers two or three choices for every course (but no substitutions). It is either handwritten on a sheet of paper inside the regular menu, or posted on a chalkboard. Look around for it.

French handwriting is a bit flowery and will take some getting used to. Even more ornate may be the restaurateur's poetic imagination, exercised with abandon when naming special dishes. Don't be embarrassed to ask for a dish to be explained to you. Your waiter expects it. It is part of his job to interpret the menu, to recommend certain dishes, and in general to exhibit his command of the cuisine he serves.

We're talking religion here. Nothing is more important to a Frenchman than what he eats. You are in a temple and your waiter is the cleric. A discussion of the menu sets the tone for the whole event and establishes a good relationship with your waiter for future visits as well.

If wine is included in the *prix fixe*, it will usually be a selection of the house wines, red, white or *rosé*. These come in a carafe, usually a quarter (*quart*), half (*demi*) or full litre (*litre*). Otherwise see the *Carte des Vins* for more choices you'll have to pay extra for. You cannot bring your own wine to a restaurant in France, but you can ask an establishment that knows you to hold your partially finished bottle of wine until the next day's meal. This is particularly convenient if you are using your hotel's dining room. Sadly, this does not hold for leftovers. You can't ask for a doggy bag. Everything is cooked fresh to be eaten immediately in France. Anyway, food portions are small.

'Anyone with any sensitivity who doesn't want to live in Paris is out of his mind.'
—American gourmet Craig Claiborne as quoted by Rudolph Chelminski in *The French at Table*

The French at table. Though space is restricted, privacy between tables is respected with lowered voices.

For those without the super French capacity for wine, drinking water along with the meal helps moderate the effects of the wine and the food. Restaurants are required by law to supply *une carafe d'eau* if requested, from the tap. But they will be much more responsive if you ask for (and pay for) bottled water. Either *avec gaz* (such as Perrier) or *sans gaz* (*plât*) like Evian and Vittel. You may have to ask for the humble carafe more than once.

Because everyone eats at the same time in France, mealtime can get frantic for your waiter, even in the poshest places. Watch that you are brought what you ordered and gently remind

'In France we don't talk about 'diets', certainly not with strangers... mainly we spend our social time talking about what we enjoy: feelings, family, hobbies, philosophy, politics, culture and, yes food, especially food (but never diets).'
—Mureille Guiliano,
French Women Don't Get Fat

him if you do end up with something you didn't ask for. He may protest (just a bit of the rooster to protest that it was not really his fault), but the error will soon be corrected. He does want you to get what you ordered.

Since restaurants in France are small, you can expect them to run out of things quickly and thus have to substitute. Occasionally, you will get a bigger carafe of wine or a more expensive dish than you wanted, so the waiter can get a bigger service (tip), which is calculated automatically as a percentage of the total bill. Usually, though, it will be an honest error, a necessary switch, or a decision on the part of your waiter that his was the better choice.

Vegetarians

If you are vegetarian, feel free to ask for a vegetarian plate even if it doesn't appear on the menu. As with most things in France, everybody loves to do something creative, something out of the ordinary, something that pushes beyond the rules. You should even try this option if you aren't a vegetarian for delightful surprises.

Desserts & Aperitifs

You will not be asked for your dessert choice until the main dishes are cleared. However, if there is a special dessert that evening which particularly appeals to you, you may ask the waiter to reserve one for you at the beginning of the meal.

After the dessert, *digestifs* such as Cognac and menthe will be offered, as well as coffee or tea. A *tisane* is an herbal tea and comes in a wide variety of flavours that can really be great if your next destination is bed. All of these will cost extra.

At the end of the meal, you must ask for the addition, which will not be brought until you make it clear you are ready to leave. To bring it sooner would be impolitely implying you should go. Some less formal places leave the bill at your table, from the beginning, tucked under a plate or table cover. They will add to that, as you order, then sum it up when you ask them to.

'A meal without wine is like a day without sunshine.'

Getting the bill is often a bit awkward. Your hosts don't want it to seem they are trying to get rid of you. Try to catch the eye of your waiter as he races past. Mimic writing on note on your hand or say a quick and quiet "*L'addition, s'il vous plaît*". Once he is sure you want it, he will bring it.

Identifying Grand Cuisine

In their endless effort to organise and qualify something as important as eating, the French have developed several systems to recognise the good, better and best restaurants in France.

The oldest and most famous, the Guide Michelin, was started by the tyre company to encourage motor-touring back in 1933. The Michelin guide comes out every year, giving one, two or three stars to the very best restaurants in France. Only a handful have three stars, and even one star puts the price out of range for most people. These restaurants must struggle hard to keep their stars, so you can count on quality, if not value-for-money. Great places to go on the expense account.

The *Gault-Millau* guides rate both restaurants and hotels. Their system is newer and a little more complex, involving a series of one to four chef's hats (*toques*) separating traditional (*toques rouges*) from *nouvelle cuisine* (*toques blanches*). There are also the Bottin Gourmand and the Auto Journal guides. Plenty of recommendations to keep you well-fed and impoverished.

Check the bill for errors. Don't be embarrassed. The French do it, too. The number '1' is often written as an inverted V in French, a bit confusing at first. The '7' is usually crossed. The tip (service) will automatically be included at 15 per cent. Leave a bit more on the table to indicate especially satisfactory service to your waiter. You don't have to leave anything extra.

Nearly everyone takes Visa or Mastercard now. Fill in the 'total' box on your credit card slip when you sign it. Be sure to say *Au revoir, Monsieur* and *Merci, Monsieur* to your waiter and the *Maître d'* when you leave.

Meeting The French Waiter Head On

The person serving you in a restaurant, (or a café, a shop or any public place) may be cool, at first, especially in Paris. This is often misinterpreted as indifference or hostility. More often it is professionalism or uncertainty, or both

What? That doesn't make sense!

Well, consider this.

A good French waiter is a proud man who wants to do his job well. He is nothing like an American kid working tables in Hollywood, just waiting to be discovered. This job is his life. He is proud of the food he serves and he wants his customers satisfied. He expects you to take your time and to take his food seriously. He is there to assist you in making a wise decision among the many options on the menu. He considers himself a professional.

But he worries: Are you just another tourist who doesn't speak French? Will he have to embarrass himself with his poor English? Probably you would prefer a quick hamburger and a coke to a proper French meal, so is he wasting his time? Or, worst of all, are you one of those officious superior Frenchmen who will treat him like a servant instead of the professional he is?

As a person new to this restaurant, you need his expertise and assistance in getting something truly delicious. Wait patiently until he can get to your table. Respect the fact that he knows you are there and he has others to serve ahead of you.

When he comes to your table (remember, always first say *Bonjour, Monsieur*), even if you can't speak much French, look the man in the eye (making him a human, your equal, not a servant) and ask for his advice. *"Qu'est-ce que vous proposez?"* (What do you recommend?)

Now, he can do his job!

WINE AND ITS PART IN FRENCH LIFE

Most of the wine drunk in France does not fall into the Grand Cuisine, AOC, categories described in the Chapter 7: The Greatest Arts of France on page 141. The stereotypical working-class Frenchman starts his day 'killing the worm' at his favourite bar or café, with a shot of basic red wine (plonk, to the English) followed by an express, the thick, bitter concentrated coffee in the tiny cup. Every bar in France serves this peculiar combination, though it's mostly the older generation that adheres to the tradition.

Except for breakfast, however, no proper French person would consider a meal without wine. From the time a child is old enough to hold a glass, he is allowed to share in the enjoyment of this beverage at family celebrations, though he must be 14 to be served legally in a restaurant.

One million Frenchmen produce nearly one quarter (US$ 22 billion) of the world's total production, yet they only export 20 per cent of that. They consume more wine, per capita, than any other people on earth except the Italians. Alcohol kills more French people than automobile accidents. It is the number three killer after heart disease and cancer.

How Wine Came to France

The Phoenicians first brought wine-making to France, trading along the Mediterranean coast. They colonised Marseilles (Marseille in French) by 620 BC, then moved inland along the shore of the Rhone River. Loving wine and planning to stay, they brought a variety of grape vines with them and planted them along their way. Some of them, like the Syrah and the Muscat, originated in Persia. All these grapes were the vinifera varieties, specifically for making wine. The Romans continued this civilising tradition, 500 years later, as they extended the Roman Empire as far as England.

All the great wines of France are made from vinifera grapes: Cabernet Sauvignon, Chardonnay, Sauvignon Blanc, Merlot, Muscat, Pinot Noir, Johannisberg Riesling and Chenin Blanc. Often these are blended together, usually in specific percentages. Until recently, the wines that resulted were known only by the name of the region in which the grapes were grown and the wine produced. Now, following the 'new world' custom, the French are naming some wines by their grape name. Alas, matching 'new world' tastes as well.

Although alcoholism is clearly a serious problem, a display of overindulgence is not acceptable. You will very rarely see a French person acting 'drunk', either at home, at a party or on the street. It puts him in the category of a 'bum'. A proper Frenchman may be a little flushed after a good midday meal, but he will not be staggering, or slurring his words, or physically ill.

How does this happen? The French have no secret of tolerance for alcohol. They consume a great deal of wine, but nearly always along with a meal. They take a glass or two each at lunch and dinner and skip cocktail hour.

Wine is not typically a cocktail in France and the cocktail party, in spite of its name, is not a Gallic institution. Before dinner at a French home or when you sit down in a French restaurant, you may be offered an *apéritif*, usually a wine-based sweet product like Dubonnet, or Vermouth (which is what the French mean when they say Martini). One regional favourite popular in Paris is a Kir: a mix of white Burgundy wine sweetened with Cassis, a blackcurrant liqueur.

Clear, sweet anise-based liqueurs like Pernod and Ricard, which become cloudy when mixed with water are Provençal favourites now offered everywhere. Otherwise, a little whisky over a piece of ice will do.

Many today just prefer a *jus d'orange* or Perrier water before the meal. For most French people, wine complements the food, not vice versa. The tannin in red wine melts the rich fats of French cuisine and blends deliciously with the meats and sauces.

Distinctive wine quality is not usually an issue of pressing importance to the French consumer. Although if you want to serve something respectable with a good meal, the AOC laws established by Napoleon guarantee a certain standard of quality, even from the most humble vineyards, that most people find satisfactory. Don't be embarrassed to just order the house wine in a restaurant.

Of course, there are 'wine snobs' who analyse every nuance and can distinguish among the years and vineyards of the great Burgundies and Bordeaux, but you'll find many more of these among the English than the French.

In fact, wine sellers in France often complain of the lack of discrimination among their countrymen. The people who pay the most for French wine are the English and the other Northern Europeans. Consequently, most of the great wines of France are sold outside the country.

Simple red wine is cheaper than beer, by the glass, in France, both in bars and restaurants. It is every man's beverage. Because drinking wine is such a basic part of everyday life in France, everyone takes it rather casually. Food rules.

A Frenchman will analyse and criticise each dish put before him, but worry not a fig over the similar subtleties of the wine served along with it. He will expect the wine to suit the food, of course, but nothing more.

This is a shame, because French wines offer a wide range of pleasing characteristics. If you know a bit about them, you will enjoy being able to pick and choose from the wine list. And finding new wines is not only fun, it is a course in French geography. Most wines are named for the places they come from in France, not the grapes from which they are made. We offer a 'tour' of France, in the next chapter, by wine region.

Learning some wines by their place names, and finding ones you particularly like, are part of the fun of being in France. Except for those *Grands Vins* of AOC which are hard to find and horribly expensive anyway, French wine is very accessible and delightfully varied in character.

Learning about the wines of France should be a light-hearted, haphazard trial-and-error experience, strictly for pleasure. There's no such thing as a 'wrong' choice for a wine with a meal. The rule of thumb is white wines with white meats (turkey, chicken, fish, veal or pork) and red wines with red meats. But you don't have to follow it. The French don't take usually their wines too seriously and neither should you.

How to Choose Wine at a Restaurant
Say you are going out to dinner at a respectable, reasonably-priced Paris restaurant. Your wine list, usually located at the end of the menu, will probably look something like this:

Vins Blancs (White Wines)
    Sancerre
    Muscadet
    Pouilly-Fuissé
    Chablis
    Vin de la Maison

Vins Rosés (*Rosé* Wines)
    Tavel
    Provence
    Vin de la Maison

Vins Rouges (Red Wines)
        Bordeaux
        Bourgogne
        Beaujolais
        Côtes du Rhone
        Aude
        Vin de la Maison

The Vin de la Maison in each category is the simplest, the house wine, and usually the least expensive of the selections. It is usually available by the quarter, half or full carafe—a full carafe being a litre container, more than one person can safely drink in a sitting.

Everything else on the list is the name of a place in France. Once you get to know the basic regional wines and learn the differences between a light red such as a Beaujolais and a heavy red such as a Côtes du Rhone, you'll have enough command to read a wine list in any but the most intimidating establishments. You can always ask the waiter for his suggestion. He'll be happy to provide it.

Most wines on the list will be sold by the bottle, though some, especially the reds, may also come by the carafe. A decent restaurant will open the bottle for you at the table, and before doing so let you look at the label to be sure it is the one you ordered.

If you order a carafe or a fraction of one, you'll have to take their word for it that they filled it with Bourgogne (Burgundy) and not just plonk. A carafe wine will usually be near the bottom of its quality category, very young, a little rough and unfinished, so the regional differences may be harder to tell.

The price of the wine usually goes up along with quality and popularity. You pay more as you become choosy about the particular wine you want to drink, especially if your favourite happens to be from the fashionable Bourgogne region. Don't go on price alone; in fact take some risks at the lower end of the prices offered, even the carafes.

There are many excellent French white wines beyond the best known, Chablis and Pouilly-Fuissé, but people know these names and order them. Consequently, they are pricey. In the more discriminating restaurants, the wine list will get more sophisticated. Here the assurances of the AOC on the label will help you. Look for the less expensive.

Most visitors (as well as the French) settle on a few regions they particularly like with particular dishes. For instance, I prefer a Bordeaux with a very good piece of meat but a Côtes du Rhone with just a steak in pepper sauce. With hearty bean soup or pasta in a tomato sauce, I'll opt for a Beaujolais or a Touraine red. With a fish course, I'll take a nice dry Muscadet over the fancier Burgundian whites.

Generally, more robust wines stand up to hearty fare. Lighter or more delicate wines are at their best with more delicately flavoured dishes. Yet, a complex wine can take either a very complex dish or a very simple one. There is nothing wrong with drinking a white or *rosé* with steak, if that's your preference! Don't be intimidated by those wine snobs, even if your waiter happens to be one.

TELLING WINES APART

So, let's start with the whites on our list, above. The differences between these wines are not great, but you may find you prefer one over another. Pouilly-Fuissé, named for a small village in Burgundy, will be the most expensive, because it has become popular as a recognisable French Chardonnay. Chablis, named for a small region south-east of Paris that is also considered part of the Burgundy region, also specialises in whites made from Chardonnay grape, but they are usually very dry and delicate, unlike a big buttery American Chardonnay.

AOC and Age

Traditionally, the better wines of France are named for the place where the grapes were grown, and those names carry real meaning. It was Napoleon who first codified wine making in his favourite wine region, the Bordeaux.

Today, in the many regions where vinifera grapes are grown, French growers are limited in the varieties they can plant, the distance apart each vine and the way they are pruned and cultivated. Likewise, wine making practices are strictly defined and controlled, including the year the wine was made.

All of this is guaranteed in the term *Appellation d'Origin Controllée* (AOC) on the bottle. This centralised micro-management creates fabulous results. The tiny vineyards of Bordeaux which produce AOC Premier Grand Cru wines can sell their better vintages for a fortune, especially as they age (and they really should). However, the value of the bottle can sometimes accelerate for years beyond the best point of development of the wine inside. Wine auctions won't guarantee the quality of their ancient, expensive vintages, and neither would I. Find an AOC red at least three years old or more and pay as little as you can for it.

One option to these is the white wines from the Loire River valley. Sancerre will be a bit fruity and may be a little spritzy, made from Sauvignon Blanc. The Muscadet will be bone dry, made in this case from the grape of the same name, but very unlike a sweet fortified American wine with the brand name Muscadet. There is a Pouilly in this region too, which is a lighter white, made from the Chasselas grape, not well known outside of France.

The house wine on our list will probably be a blend from the south of France, without an AOC and young, but drinkable with the meal, as was intended.

The *rosé* wines in France, especially those of the south (in Provence, for example) are actually the closest to those wines first made by the Romans. They are usually a blend of different red grapes, and the only reason for the light colour is that the skins are removed when the berries are first crushed.

Most red grapes have white juice. To create a red wine, the wine maker leaves the skins in the tank after the grapes are crushed and as they ferment. It is the skins that give the red colour and also much of the tannin.

Choosing a Wine with Maturity

My pet peeve about wines in restaurants, in France and all over the world, is that the reds are sold before they are fully developed. It is a waste of money to drink an expensive Bordeaux or Burgundy wine that is only two or three years old. The grapes simply haven't had enough time to mingle properly. Adding to the problem, restaurants do not always put the vintage dates of their wines on the wine list. Don't be bashful about asking for the vintage on any bottle of wine, other than the carafe wines, of course. Give a good AOC white wine at least two years and a AOC good red at least four or five years to age properly before you drink it. You will appreciate the difference.

So, in the Provençal rosé you'll find some character of a red wine, but it will be lighter and perfume-like. The *rosé* of Tavel, which is a village north of the Provence, in the Côtes du Rhone region, will have a more robust blend of red grapes. The house *rosé* will be a more simple wine, probably from the Provence but without all the requirements for an AOC.

Among the reds, you'll find a wider variety of flavours and prices. There is a constant debate between Bordeaux and Burgundy red wine lovers about which is best. They are made from different grapes. The Bordeaux wines, known as 'Claret' in England, are almost 100 per cent Cabernet Sauvignon grapes blended with 5–20 per cent Merlot, a milder flavoured red grape. The Burgundy wines are made from 100 per cent Pinot Noir grapes. Both result, in good years and with proper aging, in intense, full-bodied wines. But both take time to mature. I always ask for the year when ordering these wines. Less than three years old, and they are too green to enjoy.

The best wines of each wine region of France have been further specified by their particular village of origin, some to their particular vineyards. The Margaux wines of the Medoc region of Bordeaux, for example, can only be made from the fruit of a few specific vines near that village west of the city of Bordeaux. Same for a Meursault or a Gevrey-Chambertin from those villages in Burgundy. As a result, each has developed a certain character that some serious students of wine can distinguish, blindfolded. But even they make mistakes. This is where we leave you to plunge into the complexity of French wines for yourself.

Back to our list! The Beaujolais wines are made just in the southern part of the Burgundy region, but from a very different grape: the Gamay Beaujolais. This produces a lighter wine than the Pinot Noir. It can be drunk young. The Beaujolais Nouveau is the ultimate example of this, a wine drunk within a few weeks of harvest. But that is only sold in November and December and should be consumed cold and before the winter is over.

Properly-made Beaujolais wines are good for three years or more and are quite popular in France, with the best ones coming from the nine little villages and called the Beaujolais-Villages.

Côtes du Rhone also produces very popular wines, more intense reds than Beaujolais. The most famous of these is the Châteauneuf du Pape. All the wines of this area are made from a blend of up to nine grape varieties. These are usually a good buy in reliably hearty reds.

The Aude region is a relatively new grape growing area and has not enjoyed the prestige of an AOC designation, which delimits its vineyard practices and its grapes. However, the good hot summers in the Aude produce abundant harvests with good sugar in the grapes, so the resultant wines have good character, especially for the price. They tend to be a little fruitier and more alcoholic than other French reds, as they get more sun, so more sugar. They are usually sold very young.

THE GREATEST ARTS
OF FRANCE

CHAPTER 7

'La destinée des nations dépend de la
manière dont elles se nourissent.
(The destiny of nations depends on how
they nourish themselves.)'
—Brillat-Savarin in the 18th century

CUISINE & CHARACTER BY PAYS

Since our last update of this little book, Canadians Jean-Benoît Nadeau and Julie Barlow have taught us a new word in French. From their insightful title, *Sixty Million Frenchmen Can't Be Wrong*, I quote:

'The French word *pays* (pay-ee) doesn't translate. Literally, it means country. But inside France it refers to areas that are recognised as distinct, though they aren't delineated by legal or administrative boundaries.... '

'There are hundreds of *pays* in France... *Pays* are the spiritual countries of origin of the French—some are former kingdoms or duchies from hundreds of years ago, other are just regions around France's major cities.'

'The first thing we noticed about *pays* was how intricately they are linked to regional cuisine. The French are obsessed with their land, its geography, its history, and the traditions that sprung from it, and no matter where they end up living, their *pays* stays with them.'

One of the great delights of being in France is discovering the rich regional diversity. France has 246 kinds of cheese and each has a story worth knowing. So our thumbnail sketches of the country beyond Paris concern what they eat, what they drink. I doubt any Frenchman would protest being 'pigeon-holed' by an association with the best fare of his region, oops, his *pays*.

We can barely show a snowflake from the iceberg. Whether you are exploring the many realms of France on business or just touring, the culinary and cultural discoveries will be a constant surprise and pleasure. Keep your eyes and nose open, and ask questions. Nothing holds the interest of the French better than the topics of food and wine. For further reading I heartily recommend Anne Willan's classic *French Regional Cuisine*, my favourite source. (*See* 'Further Reading' *on page 244*).

AOC Products in France

Napoleon was the first to protect 'under law' the quality of the best of the regional food and wines. The national system of *Appellation d'Origine Contrôlée* (AOC) today recognises specific products (including wines, spirits, butter, cheese, poultry, fruit and vegetables) and guarantees both their origins and the way they are produced. When you see the 'AOC' label on a food or wine in France, you can be confident that you are getting the real thing.

The French AOC laws are among the most strict in the world. An AOC wine will not only be limited to grape juice from a specific acreage in the area named on the label. The number of vines per hectare (which is about two acres) and the way the vines are pruned each winter, the cultivation and irrigation are specified and strictly enforced.

The same detailed codification applies to many other regional delicacies. The French place great value on their culinary traditions and guard against cheap imitators. (Of course, McDonald's and Levi's also strictly standardise their products. Alas, with far less impressive results.)

Normandy

Along the coast closest to England, the Norman countryside offers simple country fare quite similar to that of England, with an emphasis on pork and potatoes, apples, cream and pastries. It is no wonder the Norman people are round and jolly. Indeed, they will remind one more of the English, with whom they have shared a common ancestry, since the Norman Conquests of 1066.

The rivers produce trout and the sea gives shellfish and saltwater fish, but like the famous soft cheeses of this region, Camembert, Pont-l'Evêque, Neufchatel and Livarot, much of the production is sold in Paris or abroad.

A thatched house near port Normandy.

Wine grapes don't grow well here, so the spirit (*eau-de-vie*) of the region, Calvados, is distilled from the popular local apple cider. *Cidre*, which is alcoholic, is a common substitute for wine at meals, and varies with every village. Benedictine, another local liqueur, is flavoured with herbs found along the Norman coast. Apple pie is the most popular dessert. With a dollop of *crème fraîche*, the French cultured cream.

Brittany

Just below Normandy, and thrust far out into the Atlantic, the rugged Breton region is most famous for its special pancakes, called *crêpes*. The local grains did not lend themselves to breadmaking, and these *crêpes* became the staple, for everything from main courses to dessert. Great sailors, the Bretons speak a language related to Cornish and Welsh. Like those early Celtic Britains, the French Bretons are an independent and self-sufficient lot.

The beloved French comic, *Asterix*, is about the misadventures of a clan of Bretons in the Roman era. It seems fighting the Romans (which they did quite successfully) and eating wild boar were the two main pastimes. The cuisine still reflects the simple dignity of the stone age monoliths called menhirs which still litter the countryside. This is also the land of the artichoke and the cauliflower, rugged individuals of the vegetable family.

For drinks, lots of *cidre* and the fine white wine of Nantes, to the south of Brittany. The Muscadet has a bone-dry simplicity that has endeared the world of wine lovers. Not fancy, but crisp and honest. Excellent with shellfish, which abound. The quatre-quarts cake, made from equal portions of flour, butter, sugar and eggs, is similar to the American pound cake.

The Loire Valley

People of the Loire Valley speak what is considered to be the purest, unaccented French, and the Loire is called the cradle of French culture. Extraordinarily known for ornate royal palaces built over the centuries, she offers a much less complicated cuisine. Plentiful fresh fish, vegetables and fruits, cooked to perfection, retain their natural character. Nothing heavy about the Loire wines and cuisine. Sophisticated simplicity.

Food writer Anne Willan explains that King Charles VIII introduced Italian vegetables to his *château* at Amboise at the end of the 15th century. These included lettuce, artichokes and green peas, formerly unknown in France. The white asparagus, so popular in spring here, never see the sun. Among fruits are plums, apples, apricots, melons, peaches and pears. From these come fruit *pâtes* in winter and fresh tarts and custard cakes in summer. Plums were brought from Damascus during the first crusade.

The wines of the region vary from the crisp, clean and dry Muscadet of Nantes to the sophisticated, slightly sparkling Saumur to the tart red Touraines to the *petillant* Vouvray. The character persevering here in both cuisine and character is a lightness and subtle sophistication quite unlike the heavier, creamier people of Brittany and Normandy.

Cointreau, the famous liqueur of Anjou, gets its flavour from orange peel. The cheeses here are Saint Paulin and baby Gouda, mild and firm, as are the goat's milk cheeses like Valençay and Sainte Maure. *Charcuteries* abound, especially game *pâté* and *rillettes*, cooked meat mixed with *pâté*.

Champagne and the North

The world's most famous sparkling wine comes from the chalk hills 160 km (100 miles) north-east of Paris. Created by monks from poor wines, real Champagne is a magic transformation, adding sugar in a painstaking second fermentation. There are wonderful sweet pastries that go along with the wine, thanks also to the vast sugar beet production. Verdun *dragées*, or sugar-coated sweetmeats, have been famous since the 13th century. The Flemish influence is also evident.

Also popular here in the north are root vegetables: carrots, potatoes, onions elevated to masterful perfection in a *pot-au-feu*. The local cabbage is transformed as well, into elegant soups, braised for hot dishes and blanched for salad. Lamb, pork and beef are also important aspects of the cuisine.

Two cheeses, the Coulette d'Avesnes and the Maroilles, are famous, and the Andouillette is a speciality. You'll find a more Northern European attitude here: more worldly. Nothing expresses this better than the success of Champagne.

This remarkable improvement on what was a rather mediocre white wine produced around Epernay was developed by a monk in the 17th century. It has enthralled the world. Almost 200 million bottles are produced each year, many of them selling for more than US$ 50 retail. The UK alone buys 10 per cent of the production and the USA just slightly less.

The Champagne-making process can be precisely reproduced now anywhere in the world, with nearly identical and much less pricey results, but aficionados will accept no substitutes. And the people of France insist. Unless the grapes were grown in the Champagne district (AOC), you cannot call it Champagne.

The Alsace and Moselle

North-eastern France, territory historically disputed with Germany, is home of the *quiche lorraine*, an egg pie that seems synonymous with French cuisine. But the staple of the region is pickled cabbage (*sauerkraut*), hot potato salad and sausage, real testimony to the Germanic heritage, as is the Alsatian language, a German dialect also spoken on the other side of the Rhine. The French influence provides dishes like their *pâté en croûte* and *mousselines*. The Alsatians will tell you they are French, not German.

Pork is also a staple, from which a wider variety of sausages are made than in Germany. There is even a 'sweet and sour' style of cooking meat with fruits here, dating back to the 16th century.

Goose is a favourite autumn dish, stuffed with apples or chestnuts. The goose liver is made into a *foie gras* that rivals that of Perigord. In fact, this region is considered the original source of forced-fed goose liver, credited to the local Jewish community, which needed a substitute for pork fat in their kosher cooking and found it in goose fat. Fresh fish is often prepared cold, *en gelée*.

The wines of the Alsace are white, dictated by the cool summers. Both dry and sweet; they are low in alcohol and are considered by some to be the best whites of France. Unlike most traditions, the wines in France are named for the grape rather than the location from which they come: Sylvaner, Riesling, Gewurtztraminer, Muscat, Pinot... Beer, of course, is the other local drink, in lighter styles than those of nearby Germany.

German-named pastries (*kugelhopf, kaffeekrautz, birewecka*), *pain de Gènes* (almond cakes), *madeleines* and the *macarons de Boulay* are all famous local desserts. Clear *eau-de-vie* is made with various fruits. Mirabelle from yellow plums, Kirsch from cherries and William pears, serve well as *digestifs* after these heavy meals. Sweet liqueurs, made from the same fruits, are recognisable for their characteristic fruit colours. They are considered medicinally beneficial.

The Münster cheese comes from a specific valley of the Vosges and gets its strength from the character of the local cow's milk. It goes well with a Gewurtztraminer.

The Alps

This region of France shares some old tribal characteristics with its neighbours, Switzerland and Italy. Hay and cattle are the crops here, so cheeses abound. Gruyère, Comté and Emmenthal, cheese fondue and cheese soufflé load the table.

The staple meat is pork, made into Chamonix ham and a variety of sausages. The fish from the streams are full of bones, so the fish meat is made into *quenelles*, or fish cakes. Many dishes are served in the gratin style, with milk and cheese. The walnuts of Grenoble are AOC, and a liqueur is made, flavoured with their flesh. Chartreuse is also from this region, a herbal liqueur flavoured with saffron, cinnamon and mace.

Wines from the Arbois are great with Morels (*morilles*), and the other wild mushrooms of the mountain forests: *girolles*, *trompettes de la mort* and *cèpes*. The rich red Rhone wines, to the south, go well with all this cuisine.

The Burgundy (Bourgogne)

South and west of Alsace, in the Soane River Valley, the Burgundy wine district begins at Dijon. The red Burgundian and Beaujolais wines are made from Pinot Noir and Gamay Beaujolais grapes, respectively. The white Chablis uses Sauvignon Blanc grapes, and the white Burgundy, Chardonnay.

In the last century, the great Burgundian wines eclipsed those old clarets of Bordeaux, adored by the English and Napoleon alike. Though Dijon and Lyon have been gastronomic centres since the 14th century when Dijon became famous for its mustard, the wines came into their own later. Now you will be lucky to find a properly aged AOC wine on the menu. The best have already been bought and put away or drunk too early.

Try the Beaujolais Village wines, each unique and very good after a year or two in the bottle. The wildly promoted *Beaujolais Nouveau*, the first wine off the press, has never appealed to me. But there is a red wine you can't drink too young.

Some local products have been transplanted, abroad. The tan Charolais beef cows, perfect for *bœuf bourguignon* and indigenous to this area, are raised all over the world, as are the famous chickens of Bresse. Wild fowl, frogs, snails and freshwater fish remain local specialities. The *escargots de Bourgogne* live in the vineyards, feasting on grape leaves all summer and hibernating under the vine roots in winter. They are usually harvested just a few weeks after they begin hibernating, when their systems are clean, but they are still plump.

From Nevers comes *nougatine*, a lovely dessert. Lyon is a chocolate haven. The sweet *crème de cassis* made from blackcurrants is the local liqueur from which the *aperatif* Kir is made. To a dry Burgundian white wine add a tablespoon of the liqueur. Among cheeses, there are the *Bleu de Bresse*, *Saint-Marcellin* and *Rigotte de Condrieu* all made from cow's milk. *Picodon* is a goat cheese from Montélimar.

The Auvergne
The centre of France is less populated than most, being the high mountains of the Massif Central. The cuisine is based on dairy products, pork, potatoes, cabbage and wild berries... real country fare. Good, strong cheeses, uncooked and pressed up in the mountains, abound: Cantal, Salers and Saint-Nectaire. Two blues, Fourme d'Ambert and Bleu d'Auvergne, are also AOC.

The Limousin oak tree here provides cooperage for Cognac and the Limousin breed of cattle gives the best of France's beef. Pork products and sausages are always popular. "Given the climate," says Anne Willan, "the cooks of the Massif Central go for calories rather than finesse ..."

People of the Auvergne have a reputation for being tight-fisted. They used to come to Paris, work in dingy cafés and save all their pennies. They have minted money with some of their products, however. The mineral waters of Perrier and Vichy spring from the mountains around the old spa towns of the same name. Badoit and Volvic are also locally produced and all are strictly controlled by their AOC.

The Limagne valley is an original source for frogs, whose legs are still fried and eaten here. So this region can be credited with giving the French another name.

Cognac and Bordeaux

South-western France, where the famous wine regions of Cognac and Bordeaux are, is a land uniquely mixed with British characteristics. In the 12th and 13th century, this Aquitaine region was part of England. The capital, Bordeaux, was the fourth largest city in England. It retains a cosmopolitan flair and remains a prosperous centre of trade.

Many still consider the Bordeaux wines unsurpassed in the world. The great Grand Cru vineyards around the city produce some of the most complex red wines from tiny AOC vineyards. Chateau Margaux, Chateau Latour, Chateau Lafite and Château Mouton-Rothschild are designated 'first-growths' of the Medoc, in the strict classification established by Napoleon himself in 1855. St Emilion has two Premiere Grand Cru. All these need ageing in the barrel and in the bottle, before they can blossom.

There are many 'surprises' as well among lesser growths of the Garonne, Dordogne and Gironde river valleys. The elegantly sweet Sauternes and the crisp dry white Bordeaux from the Graves and Entre-deux-Mers give the area a remarkable range of very distinctive wines.

Oysters on the sea coast are raised at the water's edge and brought inland to fatten and mature. They take their names from these maturing villages. The Marennes oysters have a green meat. The *entrecôte* of the Bordelaise complement the red wines, as does the St. Emilion speciality, chocolate charlotte.

The *Chabichou* goat cheese is remarkable. The Charente is both dairy country and home of Cognac, the great brandy of

France, different from an *eau-de-vie* in that, after distillation from wine, it is aged in wood barrels, instead of crocks, thus adopting a golden colour. *Foie gras* and truffles come from this area, as well as elsewhere in France, but the *truffle du Perigord* is considered the best.

The Gascogne produced Cyrano de Bergerac, the literary soul of the Frenchman: chivalrous, generous, reckless, brave, boastful and, in the end, tragic. He never gets the girl of his dreams. One supposes the men of the Bordeaux console themselves with their marvellous wines.

The Pyrénées

So far from Paris are the mountains separating south-west France from Spain, you would expect major cultural differences. And you get them. The Basque people are still demanding independence in their mountainous Spanish homeland on the south-west extreme of the Pyrénées, high above Biarritz. The local French support them.

The originators of the red beret, now a stereotype of all things French to outsiders, the Basque people have influenced the cuisine as well. Red peppers, vegetables cooked with garlic, fresh and salted fish. Once the Basque people hunted whales in the Bay of Biscay. Hot blooded adventurous people they remain.

At the bottom of the mountains, in Béarn, is the hearty country fare of a *poule-au-pot*. (The famous *béarnaise* sauce was actually invented in Paris, though named for this region.) And *confit* is another: salted meat or game cooked and preserved in fat. On the other side of the Adour river is Armagnac, home to a grape brandy aged in wood barrels, like Cognac, but ever-so slightly sweeter. They even make pastries with it.

The local cheese, *fromage des Pyrénées*, is red-skinned when made from sheep's milk and black-skinned when made from cow's. Both are AOC.

The Languedoc

Once France was divided by two languages, each indicated by the way they said 'yes'. The *langue d'oil* to the north used the word *oui* and those in the south used *oc*. Today the Languedoc includes the Mediterranean coastline, west of the Rhone river, to the Pyrenees. They are most famous for their thick bean stew *cassoulet* and *bourride*, a fish soup rich with garlic and olive oil.

The land is so rich here and the sun so plentiful, they can get three crops of vegetables, but the most important crop today is wine grapes. The Herault, Roussillon, Corbières and Minervois produce most of the basic red table wine the French love: immature and rough. This is an unfair assessment of the people, however.

In the stark, poor hills above the Tarn, sheep have been the main crop for thousands of years. Anne Willan reports a *pot-au-feu* called *cabassol* made from lamb's head and feet. Economy is still a primary consideration in much of this poor rural area, in stark contrast to the nearby city of Toulouse, now the beautiful capital of high technology in France.

The candied violets of Toulouse are a popular export item. And in the north, the Ardèche is home of the famous chestnut cream, *marrons glacés*, as well Roquefort cheese, made in limestone caves with sheep's milk and protected by law since 1411. (For the real thing, look for the little red sheep on the package.)

So what have we here? In the countryside, a simple, strong, direct farm folk and yet in Toulouse, all the sophistication of candied violets. The Languedoc has complexities you need to visit to appreciate.

The Provence

Home of the great seafood stew, *bouillabaisse*, this is a cuisine of strong contrasts: peppery, garlicky main dishes made with olive oil, and balanced with fresh, cool tomatoes (only considered edible since the 19th century), fennel and eggplants. Ratatouille was born here.

The herbs of Provence grow everywhere: lavender, rosemary, thyme, sage... add to those anchovies, olives and capers, a wild range of flavourings. Melons and figs are AOC. There is abundant evidence of Italy here, both in the cuisine and the warm, friendly ways of the people.

The lovely *rosé* of Provence is also AOC, as are the deep reds and flinty whites, The *rosé* is my favourite. Made from a blend of 12 red grapes brought by the Romans plus some varieties from ancient Persia, the juice is quickly pressed and the skins removed to give that light salmon colour. Light and full of humour, this *rosé* reminds me best of the Provençal lifestyle, as do their *aperetifs*, Pernod and Ricard. Flavoured with anise (licorice), the latter turns cloudy in water, like the outlawed absinthe and the Greek ouzo and the Arab arak. All Mediterranean.

The people of the Provencal are considered too relaxed for Parisians, who give little credence to the relaxed climate of the Mediterranean coast. But with such lovely cuisine and warm sunshine, who wouldn't spend all day at table? For more on Provence, see the films *Jean de Florette* and *Manon of the Spring*. Or read *Letters from my Windmill* by Alphonse Daudet and my favourite, *A Year in Provence* by Peter Mayle.

Ile De France (The Paris Area)

The area around Paris, for about 80 km (50 miles) in any direction, holds 20 per cent of the country's population and the vast majority of its foreign tourists. With so much going on, the visitor is apt to miss the regional specialities above. But they miss few of the raw materials. Paris has everything.

'Paris has in abundance everything that could be desired,' wrote Jerome Lippomano in 1577 (quoted by Rudolph Chelminski). 'Merchandise flows in from every country. Provisions are brought in by the Seine from Picardy, from Auvergne, from Burgundy, from Champagne and from Normandy. Thus, although the population is innumerable, nothing is ever lacking. Everything seems to fall from the sky.'

Today, this is still true. But the former market gardens around Paris have become suburban communities, and Les Halles in the centre of Paris gathers tourists, not food wholesalers. The foods of France convene now at the ultramodern wholesale market at Rungis, just south of Paris. From Rungis

much of the merchandise leaves France, flown from nearby Orly airport to gourmet capitals around the world. From New York to Hong Kong, restaurateurs call in their orders to Rungis of asparagus, oysters, wild strawberries, wild mushrooms, endive, fish, game, whatever is in season. All is flown, that same day, from Orly.

Though Paris rejoices in many culinary delights that are not original, the Ile de France has long been known for its soft cheese, the Brie, as well as fancy pastries, potatoes and endive. The *baguettes* and *croissants* that make Paris so sweet smelling, are also a regional speciality, as are *béchamel, espagnole* and *hollandaise* sauces. But just as common in Paris today are sauerkraut, couscous and pizza. Ironically, Paris is a collection of international and regional foods, many of them adapted (with a compromise of integrity in my opinion) to the local tastes. To enjoy all the true regional variety of France, both of the foods and the wines, you need to travel around the country.

Paris Wine Bars—Learning French Geography in a Glass

If you don't have time to discover the wines of France by wandering around the countryside. Or, if you return to Paris longing for more such wine adventures, you will find the 'wine bars' of Paris a happy surprise. These cafés and restaurants cater to the wine enthusiast, usually specialising in a particular region. The patron of these establishments will gather his favourite vintages. Often these are otherwise unavailable, even in a good Paris wine shop.

Usually open for lunch and all afternoon until dinner time, they offer you a happy day's 'research', often sitting out front at little tables, sipping and watching the Parisians go by. With selections by the glass, you can compare the nuances of neighbouring villages or different years, as well as the range of reds and whites. Plates of fresh country breads with a selection of local charcuterie or cheese will be served, too, so you can enjoy the way the various wines complement the foods of the region. It is adventure travel for the palate.

However, you will need a nap before dinner.

THE OTHER ARTS
French Film: C'est du cinéma

The French have an idiom, *C'est du cinéma*, which loosely translates to: 'That's not real', or 'It's unbelievable'. While it is reassuring to know that the French distinguish between fantasy and reality, the significance of *le cinéma* and *les cinéastes* (film makers) is profound.

The French are absolutely gaga about *les films*. Both *Pariscope* and *L'Officiel*, the competing weekly schedules for Paris films, can be found in nearly everyone's pocket. There are literally hundreds of films showing at any one time in Paris and English language films are often shown in V.O. (*version originale*) which means the original language with French subtitles.

As an art form, film is not SO far behind gastronomy in the hearts of the French. The *cinéastes* work with natural ingredients: people, places, feelings, things, colours,

'C'est du cinema.' Say the French, but, oh my, they love the films.

textures to create a grand artifice, which the French consumes as if it were as real as pastry, as tangible as life.

C'est du cinéma, the idiom admonishes us. Yet we are convinced. Film is another kind of reality and there is something distinctly French about French films. They differ in the design and strategy of their presentation, in their evident intention and in their attention to certain topics and themes.

French films offer endless and wonderful insights into the French psyche and French values.

French Art

Picasso warned us: 'All art is a lie'. I would be lying not to admit that my enthusiasm for the arts does not centre around museums. Since there are libraries on the subject of French art and the museums of Paris are world renown, I just offer the briefest historical review here. Get ye to the museums to learn more!

In the 16th century, the Renaissance came to France from Italy. The discovery of the world beyond Europe and the Middle East, the rediscovery and development of the sciences and the invention of the printing press in Germany all created an intellectual explosion across Europe. King François I invited gifted Italian artists of the day to France. Leonardo da Vinci (who actually died in France), Benvenuto Cellini and Titian decorated his new castle at Fontainebleau so magnificently that other wealthy landowners took up the trend. The fabulous chateaux sprinkled along the Loire river valley remain. In 1546, this King began the 'new' Louvre castle and the Tuileries in Paris, built upon the foundations of city fortifications going back to Roman times.

By the 17th century, Paris counted among the great cultural capitals of Europe. Under the direction of Cardinal Richelieu, the streets were paved and the Ile St Louis and Marais filled with magnificent hotels, city homes of the wealthy, both aristocrats and the new merchant class. The Luxembourg palace and gardens were completed on the left bank, the Louvre enlarged and gilded. Louis XIV built Versailles into a magnificent central point of royal power—economically, socially and physically. Here, he kept his nobles in splendid confinement, encouraging their petty infighting and squabbles to prevent their gathering force against him.

In the countryside, artists such as Georges de la Tour and the brothers Lenain depicted the simple peasant and his work. They reflected the new value of humanism that became the foundation of the democratic principles on which France stands today.

The turbulent politics of the 18th century brought a decline in both the decorative arts and in individual expression. Art and architecture became a function of politics. The old Bastille prison was torn down and its stones used to build the bridge at the Place de la Concorde. The people could then walk across the Seine, on this symbol of oppression, and up the steps of their Assemblée Nationale, one of two representative legislative bodies that still today sets laws according to the will of the people.

The symbol of this new France became the young, bare-chested peasant woman, fondly called Marianne, holding the tricolour flag. (It deserves future discussion that Marianne today is the face, but not the bare breast, of movie star Catherine Deneuve.)

By the second half of the 19th century, three schools flourished: the romantic painters such as Delacroix and Gericault; the realists, Ingres and Courbet and the symbolist, Corot, precursor of France's greatest contribution to the arts. The next generation, Monet and Renoir, led this new artistic

From the *quai* to the Louvre, artists still abound in Paris.

force called Impressionism. Art historians now credit the sunlit ripples of the painting *The Seine at La Grenouillère* as the first Impressionist painting, done in 1869.

Monet and Renoir were soon joined by Camille Pissarro, Degas and Cézanne. The next generation included Georges Seurat and Paul Gauguin, then Henri Matisse, Pablo Picasso (Spanish, but adopted by the French), Paul Klee (Swiss-German) and Georges Braque.

Paris became the romantic home of a romantic lifestyle: the ultimate individual, the artist. After food and politics, nothing tickles the French middle-class sensibility more quickly than 'art'. That includes all the media, visual, fashion and film. Artists are adored, though they have to struggle quite a bit for attention, with so many others around. A person who cares nothing for art is considered uncivilised in France, no matter what his other attributes might be.

Visit an art exposition in Paris, especially an opening, or *vernissage*. It will be teaming with the artifice of the arts. The beautifully dressed will be plentiful, even while the artist may be that dishevelled guy slouching embittered in the corner. All part of the show. There is so much of artistic merit in everything about French life, I consider every Frenchman something of an artist, and all of France his canvas. And that's no lie.

Sensuality and Sex

Well, we have to put this somewhere and certainly sensuality is one of the enjoyable arts of France. Sex, that is its expression in the differences between the sexes, is a constant source of entertainment to the French. Their fascination with the subject and their expertise in conveying that passion is apparent everywhere in Paris. Sensuality spills from the magazine stands, the advertising billboards and the shop window displays.

This is not to say that French women are loose or that love is free. But the French love to do one thing and that they do very well. They flirt. And if you relax just a little, you will find yourself enjoying the constant flirtations going on around you. You will even find yourself flirting, too.

The Pigalle section of Paris still draws busloads of tourist and sensuality abounds all over town.

The act of sex is not the goal of this sensual game. It is rather a celebration of the differences. It is an art form. (An actual sexual climax in French is called *la petite mort*, or the little death.)

Sometimes, of course, flirtation goes farther. Extramarital affairs exist in France as well, but rarely cause a divorce or the loss of a job. Everyone knows that two women followed Mitterrand's *courtége,* his wife and his mistress.

'Polygamy is the opposite of monotony' goes the French saying and monotony is to be avoided at all costs, as we know from Mademoiselle Chanel. Marriage and the family are quite strong institutions in France, well defined both by the Roman Catholic Church and the Napoleonic Code.

Marriage involves many more economic expectations but fewer personal ones. Such life partners are not joined at the hip and each has his own interests. Most of the time, they share the pleasures and the responsibilities of their children and their extended families.

While women do not share an equal presence with men in the halls of business and politics, their presence is always appreciated and their individuality respected. If you are a man, you will quickly find out why if you ever approach a provocatively dressed French woman without proper decorum. As a woman, you can expect to be treated with respect in France and should openly condemn anyone who doesn't.

Sex For Money

Prostitution was declared illegal in 1946, just around the time that women in France finally got to vote! Visit the Pigalle district on any night of the year and you will think the world comes to Paris for sex. A wide variety of sexual pleasures are promoted (and to some degree satisfied) in Paris. It is to be expected, given the general enthusiasm of the French for all things sensual.

Predictably, the French don't make a particularly clear distinction between the joys of food, fashion and sex. A major resource on sex in Paris, a book called *Paris La Nuit Sexy*, devotes most of its pages to descriptions of the restaurants in town. (Which is why we put this topic in the 'culture' section of this book.)

Certainly, if you aren't interested in prostitution, you can avoid it. But you can't avoid the sensuality!

The big reviews, the *Grands Spectacles* at places like the Lido, Crazy Horse Saloon, the Moulin Rouge and the Paradis Latin are designed for wowing tourist groups from Birmingham, Hokkaido and Iowa. You won't find them shocking beyond nudity. For some real titillation, you'll have to go to the erotic shows such as Théâtre des 2 Boules and Théâtre Saint-Denis or a chain of peep-shows around Paris designed for that.

Homosexuality is called 'the English vice' in France, but there's lots of playing around with variations on the conventional themes here. The most discreet, anonymous way of participating in sexual games is by modem. Use your Minitel, the French computer that comes with telephone service, to link up with these services.

Tap a code (try AC1, there are hundreds) and someone on the other side starts answering or asking questions on your screen. You can type replies as you like (there are even English language ones) because nobody knows who or what you are. Totally anonymous. Perfect for fantasising, and you just pay via your telephone bill.

The next step up, in terms of active participation, is the erotic telephone numbers. For these you'll need a bit more French. For face-to-face, there are certain bars, discotheques and dance halls. Some of these specialise: gay or lesbian sex, couples exchanges, S&M. These are usually 'pick-up' places. If your French is poor, be sure to bone up on your non-verbal skills.

More intimate still are the clubs (*clubs de rencontres*) and saunas which open from 10:00 pm to 7:00 am, where your participation will be expected. There are also women 'at home' you can call directly. The Minitel access number or the book mentioned earlier in this section will give you a directory of them. Thanks to the liberated French telephone company (run by the Government) you can let your fingers do the walking...

Where you shouldn't walk, especially at night, is in the stunning old Bois de Boulogne, the immense woods on the western edge of Paris. This is where the weirdest action is. Fortunately for the families who would also like to enjoy this park, most of the sexual action is limited to specific areas for specific purposes at specific times of day. There is actually a map which indicates what is going on where. But it isn't posted in public places.

Much of the 'pick-up' process and ultimately the activities themselves are done in cars. Avoid walking off into the woods around the Lac Inférieur in the early evening, even in summer when it is light until 10:00 pm. The woods are literally littered with action.

There are many other locations for good old, straight-forward, pay-as-you-go prostitution in Paris, where there are said to be 20,000 full-time prostitutes and another 60,000 working part-time. (I don't know how they conduct the census.) Basic price is 25 euros a throw (plus the hotel, if you're not in the Bois). The basic locations are fairly obvious: the train stations of Montparnasse, Gare du Nord and Gare de l'Est, the Pigalle and the Boulevard Clichy (both straight and gay), and around Les Halles.

For rock-bottom prices, try Porte de la Chapelle in the *10ème*, rue Chalon in the *12ème* and rue Houdon in the *18ème*. Higher prices and better quality can be found at the Pyramids *métro* (and nearby rue Sainte Anne for gays) and at the Avenue de la Grande Armée and Porte Maillot, not far from the Bois. Here prices jump to 50 to 75 euros. The Saint-Germain-des-Prés area in the 6ème is mostly for gay services. Even in Paris, there are still few opportunities for straight women to buy men's sexual services. One would assume there are just not many paying customers.

THE YEAR'S HOLIDAYS AND SEASONS

Like most Europeans, the French write their dates numerically, starting with the day, then the month, then the year.

The official summer holiday in France starts on Bastille Day, 14 July, and goes through the end of August. Paris is very quiet that month; there won't be opera and other major cultural events, only the usual tourist sights. However, the Mayor of Paris puts on special events during the summer to compensate for this, but there won't be any major traffic jams. Conversely, expect the seaside resorts and country camping grounds to be packed to the gills.

In early September, schools begin and everyone returns to their routine. In October, usually the best month for good weather, Paris is jammed with all sorts of special events and conferences. Hotels will be booked up and restaurants will require reservations.

On the major holidays, the banks and post offices will close and the long weekend will lure many families out on the highway. Fatalities rise so sharply during these periods that the government has tried to spread out the school holidays more evenly—scheduling six weeks of school followed by two weeks' holiday.

If a national holiday falls on a Tuesday or Thursday, many companies will *faire le pont* (make a bridge). This means they will include Monday or Friday as part of the holiday as well, thus creating a four-day weekend. Take note not to plan business meetings on these days.

Cultural Holidays, Festivals and Notable Events

- **6 January**
  La Fête des Rois (Epiphany)
  Epiphany was originally a religious festival celebrating the visit of the Magi to Jesus. Today, the popular custom is to hide a small figurine inside a cake (*galette des rois*). The cake is then cut into pieces and distributed among the members of the family. The person with the figurine in his piece will be king or queen for the day. *Galettes des rois* can be found in *boulangeries* throughout the week of the festival.

- **February**
  Mardi Gras
  Also known as Carnaval, the celebrations vary depending upon which part of France you visit. In several cities, such as Dunkerque, the traditional costume parade is still held.

- **March**
  Foire du Trône
  A temporary fairground is set up in the Bois de Vincennes in Paris, with rides and activities for children.

- **End of April**
  La Foire Internationale de Paris
  A large week-long fair held in Porte de Versailles, with vendors selling everything from furniture to food.

- **May**
  French Open Tennis Championship
  Also known as Roland Garros, this is the event that has the biggest names in professional tennis come to Paris each year to compete. It's the only major tennis championship held on clay courts.

List of Official Holidays

1 January   **Jour de l'an (New Year's Day)**
New Year's Eve is usually celebrated with friends, fireworks and parties. The Eiffel Tower and Champs Elysées are two of the more popular places to be for the big countdown.

March/April   **Lundi de Pâques (Easter Monday)**
A religious holiday. Children usually have an Easter egg hunt.

April/May   **Ascension (Ascension Thursday)**
A religious holiday, observed on the sixth Thursday following Easter.

May/June   **Pentecôte (Pentecost)**
A religious holiday. Second Monday following Ascension.

1 May   **Fête du Travail (Labour Day)**
An celebration of workers' rights.

8 May   **Victoire 1945 (French Liberation Day)**
Commemorated with a veterans' parade in celebration of the end of WWII.

14 July   **Fête Nationale (Bastille Day)**
Fireworks and parades are held in the streets on Fête Nationale, in celebration of the French Revolution. There is also La Balle de Quatorze Juillet, an evening dance held outdoors throughout France.

15 August   **Assomption (Assumption)**
A religious holiday.

1 November   **La Toussaint (All Saint's Day)**
Traditionally, people bring flowers to the graves of their ancestors.

11 November   **Armistice 1918 (Veteran's Day)**
A day held in remembrance of those who fought in World War I

25 December   **Noël (Christmas)**
Christmas is usually celebrated with an extended family dinner (usually starting at 10:00 pm) on Christmas Eve. Gifts are exchanged on Christmas Eve or Christmas Day.

- **21 June**
  Fête de la Musique
  An outdoor music festival held in celebration of summer. Musicians from all over the world descend upon France to play in the streets. Make sure you bring an instrument!
- **July**
  Tour de France Cycling Championship
  The famous three-week cycling race across France. For information on the current year's route, go to: http://www.letour.fr
- **Mid-September**
  Les Journées du Patrimoine
  This is observed throughout the country with historic landmarks being opened to the public for free. This includes buildings usually closed to the public, such as le Palais de l'Elysée (residence of the President of France).
- Mid-October
  International Contemporary Art Fair (FIAC)
  Some of the greatest contemporary art works, which are privately owned, are put on display at the FIAC. Some may be available for sale.
- **Mid-November**
  Beaujolais Nouveau
  This is the time when the Beaujolais nouveau is officially distributed for sale throughout France. Many people go out to cafés or restaurants to celebrate and savour the much-loved French wine.

PARLEZ-VOUS FRANÇAIS?

CHAPTER 8

'Language is a national complex in France...
They love and cherish their language in ways
that are almost incomprehensible to the English
speakers. It is their national monument.'
—*Sixty Million Frenchman Can't Be Wrong*

THE ART OF CONVERSATION

Innate restlessness and a love of diversity are both satisfied by lengthy conversation in France, usually in the structure of analysis. Everywhere you go, the French are analysing life. Sometimes this is on a pretty mundane level, but whether you are passing time talking politics in a café or just buying envelopes, expect a discussion of the options.

Even with my 'mini' French, I have learned amazing details about envelopes, their sizes and their various glues, just by listening in, or asking the salesperson's opinion myself. Be it the choice of stationery, the fruits in season or world politics, contrast and detail challenge the French intellect and heighten everyone's self-esteem.

The French love nothing better than to be asked their opinion on a subject. And it is remarkable how many topics they feel strongly about. Happily, there is no particular need for you to agree. The discussion is the relevant thing. And more than one point of view is encouraged, otherwise, what is the point?

Compromise has negative meaning in France. It is to be avoided. It is far better to end a discussion with all points made than find some pathetic bit of common ground to stand together on, casting most of our own ideas in the dust. You don't have to try for consensus.

The French are quick to criticise everybody and everything, but that is often only to open a discussion. Most good conversations start with a complaint and end with a satisfactory display of analytical thinking. Remember: thesis, antithesis, synthesis.

Waiters love to discuss the nuances of their menus, plumbers the fine points of their trade, and businessmen the extent of their understanding of the workings of the world. You should be willing to participate.

People who complain that the French talk too much are probably the same ones who say the French are cool and uncommunicative. They miss the point, both times. The art of conversation in France is highly developed. It follows very specific rules. But as a foreigner with limited skills in French, you will be forgiven a multitude of sins, as long as you don't commit the only cardinal sin: refusing to join in.

The Art of Rhetoric

'The art of rhetoric is so alien to North American culture that few people even understand what it is. But rhetoric is the treasured art of the French. Rhetoric is not the mere science of persuasion and oratory. It is the art of eloquence, whether in writing or in speech.'

'The French learn to value and practice eloquence from a young age... now they follow a dialectic model of thesis-antithesis-synthesis... they present an idea, explain possible objections to it and then sum up their conclusions...'

'This analytical mode of reasoning in integrated into the entire school corpus.'

—*Sixty Million Frenchmen Can't Be Wrong*
by Jean-Benoît Nadeau and Julie Barlow

SILENCE AND ITS PRESERVES

Before we go further, please note that silence can be very appropriate in France, especially among strangers. Silence preserves, the French say. It allows polite distance between people in a public place. Neighbours in a building may respect each other's privacy by maintaining silence as they wait together on the ground floor for the lift (but only after they have acknowledged each other with a *Bonjour, Madame* or *Monsieur*). They may go no further in their relationship for years. But once that barrier is broken, the talk never stops.

In a train compartment with six seats, silence will be maintained among all the passengers after acknowledgement of their presence (*Bonjour...*). If there is a conversation between two friends among the six, it will conducted as quietly as possible, out of respect for the others' privacy, i.e. their right to silence.

Silence and an expressionless face are neutral in France, not cold. Americans are taught to smile, no matter what. The French are taught to honour other people's privacy, and their own, with detachment. Reserve. They smile only when there is a reason.

In line at a grocery store, if the wait is long, a French person may make body motions indicating their impatience. He may throw a look of exasperation at other customers in the line for confirmation of the situation, but he will almost never speak. He would certainly not strike up a conversation with his queue neighbours and discuss some intimate detail of his personal life.

Beyond Bonjour Monsieur

While silence preserves, it is not appropriate between acquaintances. To pass a person you know on the street or bump into other parents at pick-up time at school without exchanging a small conversation would be considered rude in France. Just *Bonjour, Monsieur* is not enough. A few comments about some topic of interest you share in common, sensitive to the time limitations of each of you, is expected. The same goes when exchanging business with a shopkeeper you know well. Ask *Ça va?* at least, and wait for their reply.

Silence Between Friends

As conversation implies a degree of commitment to the other person, the closer you are to another person, the less silent you would expect to be in their presence. Silence between friends might imply indifference. Often friends will sit in a car or a café together and chatter away on some trivial matter. They might just be avoiding the lonely distance that silence might bring. It is a kind of mutual support system.

Starting Conversations With Strangers

French conversation in public among strangers is usually limited to exchanges between customers and shopkeepers. To go into a café and start talking to another customer could easily be an invasion of his or her privacy, or even misunderstood as a proposition on your part.

Conversation commits people. So make your advances gingerly. You'll find plenty of seemingly 'non-communicative' French people happy to talk to you, with the proper approach. The French are most at ease when they are in conversation. They love to express their opinions. They just need the appropriate opportunity to get started.

'Everything can be seen from several angles and in several lights.'
—Montaigne

Your best bet at a bar or in a café or shop is to wait until other customers have been presented to you through the waiter, bartender or clerk. If you are with a group, or they are, that makes your advances easier, as your motives are clearly innocent.

People sitting at a table next to you may themselves start a conversation with you, especially if you are alone. Once they realise you are from another country a different point of view, ah ha! What an opportunity for discussion!

'In another language, you not only say things differently, you say different things.'
—Joseph Barry,
The People of Paris

Answer their question or comment in French if you possibly can. Show your willingness for further conversation by offering observations on the same or a different topic.

The main topics to avoid are: a person's age, what he does for a living and how much money he makes. Americans note: the very 'ice-breaker' question that starts most conversations in American, "What do you do?" is strictly none-of-your-business in polite conversation in France, even at private parties among friends.

Speak Softly, Especially in English

Whatever you talk about, especially in public spaces, remember to moderate your voice! Even a normal volume, in a shop or at a restaurant, will disturb others and will be considered very rude.

The French love to talk, but they are extremely courteous of other people's desire for silence (and privacy) in public places. No one but your interlocutor should be aware you are speaking. This is easier to remember when you are alone.

Most of us who travel have been embarrassed by our fellow countrymen speaking too loudly in their own language. Having one or more of your own countrymen along with you anywhere puts you into a little cultural 'bubble' of your own. Suddenly, the culture around you doesn't count.

Remember to moderate your voice. And remind your friends or your partner. That is the golden rule of conversation in France.

So, what are you going to talk about? Ideas! The French are well-informed about world politics, history and the arts. They will have opinions and they will be interested in yours.

Your most important preparation as a conversationalist, besides learning the language itself, will be a willingness

Lively conversation, including the hands, is a favourite activity for all ages.

to analyse world politics, art and culture. Be interesting, be amusing, be yourself.

Incendiary questions about politics are perfectly acceptable here. You can take any position you want, you can criticise anything you feel strongly about, but be ready to distinguish between something you don't understand and something you can argue clearly.

The point of conversation is batting around ideas and perhaps learning something. It is not about winning an argument. The important thing is not to get 'stuck' in your own ideas. Be willing to accept new reasons for old observations. Studying culture, your own, or anyone else's, takes a perpetually open mind. Remember, thesis, antithesis, synthesis.

Conversation as a Dance or Drama

French conversation has elements of the dance and drama. The most popular television programme in Paris for years was a literary talk show called *Apostrophe*. They did nothing but provide interesting analysis of the issues of the day. Raymonde Carroll likens Frenchconversation to a spider's web. A good one is made up of many different threads and angles, creating a beautiful and complex shape at its end. It is unnecessary, in fact, undesirable, to seek a common point of view. This is less difficult for the English, accustomed to the art of debate than it is for Americans, who normally offer agreement just to be polite. If you find a French person who speaks English to you, you still want to follow the rules of French conversation.

- Seek topics that will interest your listener.
- Keep your commentary lively, animated and brief. Don't turn a question into a lecture, holding the floor. It is rude and worse, it is boring.
- Don't make a conversation as an opportunity to unload your personal problems. Make it an amusing or horrible incident, if you must focus on your own life. And keep it short, with some point other than your own personal history to be made.
- Let the focus of the conversation move around to different topics. Each person should contribute little snatches of comment, tossing the conversation back and forth, like a ball.
- You can change the subject. But some logical transition is usually expected. In a restaurant, you can always talk about the food (a favourite topic and fine ice-breaker).
- Other good subjects include current events or a recent incident that gave you an insight worth relating. Try to offer something constructive and enlightening. In other words, THINK. And give your conversation partners the benefit of that effort.

- As the ball goes back and forth, keep acknowledging the speaker, with little sighs or nods of agreement. (There is a special way the French say *Oui*, while sucking air in, that is a popular way of doing this.) Show yourself to be listening attentively. If you are getting bored, change the subject when it is your turn.

- Interruptions are perfectly acceptable in French conversation. One French conversant need only give the slightest pause for the other to cut in with his response. If you don't give a pause, your French interlocutor will probably break in. That's not being rude, that's being participatory. The rapidity of the interruptions and even the volume of the exchange may increase as everyone gets more excited—like a dance that gets faster and faster. Just remember not to disturb others around you.

- A lively conversation is a successful interaction. As intensity builds, burst of laughter and even explosions of anger may occur. Don't be alarmed. Drama is part of the debate, and the quest is only for a better understanding of the topics covered and a deeper respect for the intelligence of the individual players involved. A frenzy of disagreement may suddenly collapse into a new subject; the pace changes, the players move on.

- I have been involved in heated and interesting debate with people I have met on a train or in a café. But your best chance of good conversation with the French is a table. Animated conversation happens often with friends in restaurants, or at a dinner party. Watch a few of them quietly to see how they play. The original meaning of *converser* in French was 'to live with some one'. There is a delicious intimacy established with good conversation. That is why the French consider it so important and make so much of it.

CONVERSATIONAL CONFRONTATIONS WITH STRANGERS—THREE RULES

From Chapter 3 you will remember that not every conversation with a stranger will start out as polite and friendly banter. Perhaps because it is so awkward to break through that polite barrier of silence with strangers, the French have perfected the *engueulade*, or argument.

A negative comment serves to get the conversation started, to force the other fellow to get involved. There are several reasons this is often acceptable behaviour. First, any recognition of a stranger is bringing him into a circle of privacy. The mere fact the person is taking off his public mask of indifference to get into conversation establishes a form of intimacy. Criticism is popular in France because it allows the other person to then give his point of view without appearing too intimate. Criticising is not the same as insulting.

There may well be a parent/child relationship at work here. He is thereby taking responsibility for you, as a person. In this case, discussion is not expected on your part, but attentiveness. Show you are *bien élevé* (well-raised). Accept the criticism and thank the speaker for his generous display of concern.

The French do not usually like to appear at fault. They don't mind being mistaken, being educated and becoming better informed. But never lay the blame for a situation upon someone else. Instead, seek solutions to the problem together.

Enjoy the *engueulade*!

IN FRANCE TRY TO SPEAK FRENCH

You miss a great deal, not speaking some French in France. Criticism is a way of getting to the heart of the matter here, and nothing of significance happens without lengthy discussion and deliberation. Speaking the language, even at a minimal level, will be enormously helpful to you in gaining respect.

Muster up your linguistic courage and plunge in. Your bad grammar and poor vocabulary will be forgiven more easily than the smile of the deaf/mute. Paris entertains more ingenue, ill-prepared travellers than any other city on earth and it is a tribute to the true humanitarian spirit of Parisians that so many confused, dumb, rude, loud and lost souls are accommodated. The least you can do is try to speak their language.

You will not be expected, as a mere foreigner, to speak French well, but you will be encouraged, from the first word, to keep trying. And you will complimented for your efforts. Start with simple things: the numbers, polite phrases, and the spelling of your name in the French alphabet. Remember Polly Platt's Ten Magic Words: '*Excusez-moi de vous déranger, Monsieur (Madame), mais j'ai une problèm...*' That gets the French every time. Under that cool reserve, they really want to help.

THINKING LIKE THE FRENCH

As you get to know the language better, you will soon find a separate reality to the French language. It is not just a way of speaking, but also a way of thinking.

- **M / F**

  The most obvious difference is that French, like other Romance languages, includes a sexual element missing in English. All French nouns are either masculine or feminine and the articles and adjectives must agree. Is it the language that makes the French so conscious of sex or the other way around? Who knows, but learning the gender of French nouns will keep the differences more firmly in your mind.

- **TU / VOUS**

  Another characteristic always paramount in French is the relationship between the speakers. The second person singular, *tu/toi*, is reserved for close friends and family members of the same age and younger. The more formal second person form, *vous*, and its agreeing verb forms are used otherwise. Even in the more informal society of today, *vous* is used in the way hip teenagers speak to adults.

- **M / MME / MLLE**

  The formality of the way a person is addressed is also important. *Madame* or *Monsieur* and a person's title, such as *Monsieur le directeur*, are used to address a business associate who is your superior. Until you know a person well, use their last name to address them, along with *Monsieur, Madame or Mademoiselle* and the *vous* forms.

Mademoiselle is used with girls too young to be reasonably married (*Mademoiselle* Chanel was an exception). As you become better acquainted, your French friends and colleagues will ask you to switch to first names, but they will expect you to continue with *vous*.

Only when friendships are really established, should you begin using the *tu/toi* and it should never be used with your elders or superiors. You can imagine how this language distinction regiments relationships.

- **NOUNS vs VERBS**

French is also a more nominal language, while English is more verbal. That means that nouns in French are more important. Nouns categorise things, an important aspect of French thinking and planning. Verbs are more important in English because action is so primary to Anglo-Saxon thinking. Direction of action is secondary.

The French will often devise an intricate Grand Plan before taking any action. The star patterns of the roads of France mean you don't want to start off on the wrong foot. It may take our French speaker a great deal of ruminating, including many meetings with colleagues, to devise his plan. He will talk it over with everyone first, considering every possibility, before he takes action.

When a Frenchman does take action, usually his goal is set. Consequently, the direction of the action is usually built into French verbs. In English, it tends to be tacked on as an adverb or preposition. For example, we go down or up the stairs. In French, *il descend l'escalier or il monte l'escalier*. Same stairs. Different verb.

As you learn the language, don't overlook the beauty of the language itself! Listen to the way the French speak, the musicality. Imitate them. Use their inflections and tones. You'll soon get it. And they will love you for it.

FAUX AMIS

There are certain words you will learn that are false-friends in French. They do not mean the same thing in French and English, although they look the same. Here are a few of them:

adorer	to adore (in French, is only the third degree of 'to like')
aimer	to love (in French this really means 'to like')
detester	to detest (really mean to 'dislike')
brésilien	transsexual
car	bus (not automobile)
composter	to validate a train or bus ticket
correspondance	to change train lines (also has the English meaning)
dame âgée	older woman (a term of respect in French)
demander	to ask (not 'to demand')
location	to rent
sortie	exit

A major stumbling block with Parisian French is the *argot* or slang words that young people are thinking up all the time. Even the books on the subject quickly become obsolete. Start spending time with teenagers. That's the best way to learn 'in' (*branché*) French.

APPRENDRE!

In French, to learn and to teach are rendered by the same verb, *apprendre*. Children know this instinctively and they have little trouble with either. Though we cannot say learning French is painless, much work has been done on teaching methods. Summarising a lifetime in language and linguistics, John Dennis, professor at San Francisco State University, offers his helpful approach to French language learning.

Au Secours! (Help)

In a well-known American film, a young, cheerful student of about 19 has failed his entrance examinations into a prestigious American university. His exasperated father hires an outrageously attractive woman to tutor him, her payment based on his passing the exam. The subject at hand? French grammar.

In the occasional scenes where anything remotely academic occurs, we see the young man stumbling through the present tense of *être,* the verb 'to be': '*Zhuh swee, too (um) ess, ill (ah) ess – est – er? ell est...*'

His pronunciation is appalling, but never mind, we admire his progress, both with French and with the tutor, as romance springs between them and becomes the major part of the film, implying that pillow talk is perhaps the best way to develop a language skill. In the end, the young man passes his exam, the tutor is rewarded handsomely and the viewer is left with a variety of misconceptions about the French language and learning a foreign language, in general.

Excusez-moi... (Excuse Me...)

Here are the false assumptions in the film:
- French is an inherently difficult language.
- French grammar is more complex than the grammar of other languages.
- Success in learning to speak French depends on mastery of French grammar.
- French pronunciation presents problems because the French language has more sounds than other languages have.
- The methodology of teaching French as a foreign language depends basically on the ability of non-native speakers to memorise and to reproduce exactly.
- Native speakers of French tend to speak so rapidly that foreigners can't understand them.
- French is the language of love/diplomacy/logic.

All these ideas are wrong. The only truth about the film was: pillow talk is one way to learn to communicate in any language. If that is not among your options...

Ecoutez-moi (Listen Up)

A great deal of your success or failure in learning a foreign language depends on your attitude towards the language and the capabilites you assume for yourself, as a language learner. Let's try to set things straight. To put it simply, either you take charge of yourself and the language you intend to learn, or it takes charge of you, which means you are overwhelmed and fall back on the excuses exposed above. As adults, we don't have the opportunities that we had as children when we acquired a native language. For the first three years of our lives, learning a language was our major activity. Learning another language, later on, is quite a different experience.

When we learned our mother tongue, we had no options. With a new language, we have to have a motive, an answer to the question, 'Why do I have to do this?' The answers vary, but one thing is clear: it is most unlikely that the language you begin as an adult will ever approach the dimensions of your native language. This should relieve some of your anxiety and help to simplify your task. Some other words of support:

- No language is inherently difficult. Native languages are more or less as difficult as foreign languages, depending on the native language(s) of the learner.
- The same applies to grammar.
- Learning to speak a foreign language depends primarily on one's desire to speak, then on one's need to say certain things, on one's ability to imitate new or modified sounds with accuracy, and on one's choice of vocabulary and structures to present the messages. To put grammar first, is to confuse the grammar of a language—it's anatomy, so to speak—with the language itself, which consists of more than grammar (as a person is more than his anatomy).
- The other four ideas on the previous page are *bêtise*, either patently untrue or unsound judgements. Subscribing to any of them will inhibit your ability to learn any language.

Montrez-moi (Show Me)

Without attempting a substantial analysis of the distinctive features of the French language, we can point to certain things that make French seem strange and difficult to learn.

- The sound system of French contains 15 vowels, four of which are nasalised, produced through the nose instead of through the mouth. Of the remaining eleven vowels, three are uncommon in other languages. The '**r**' sound in French is a distinctive 'scrape' and takes a good deal of practice to reproduce accurately.

- There is a way of connecting words through linking the last sounds of one to the first sound of another: *Il est-t-arrivé.*
- There is a practice of stressing the final syllable of words in French: incroyABLE instead of inCREDible.
- For the literate learner of spoken French, there are more than a few instances of silent letters: *homme, sable, fort, sous, tabac, difficile.* These silences occur in the beginning, middle and end of the words.
- The two most common problems cited by learners are these: Gender—the use of the articles *la, le, l'* and *une, un.* Complements of verbs—the use of prepositions after verbs: *vernir à* or *de, décider à* or *de, promettre à* or *de.*

Verb tense, aspect and mood are also somewhat mystifying, especially the subjunctive. Vocabulary can be easily sorted out into a list determined by frequency of use, which ranges from high-frequency words such as articles, prepositions and pronouns, to the generic verbs (come, go, wait, buy, think, see, etc.), the generic nouns (numbers, house, market, bread, fruit, meat, etc.) and attributes (left, right, large, small, good bad, expensive, cheap, etc.)

When learning French in a country where French is spoken, you have the advantage of observing cultural behaviour, as well. The relationship between what one says and how one says it (intonation of speech and body gesture), where and when one can say it, all should be integrated into any language learning experience. The culture needs to be learned and understood along with the language.

Apprenez! (Learn! Teach Yourself!)

The list of obstacles to the learner of French is neither lengthy nor formidable. The French verb *apprendre* can mean both learn and teach because they are two sides of the same coin.

For pronunciation, you will need an excellent model, preferably a native speaker. Not only must your pronunciation be intelligible, it must be accurate 95 per cent of the time! For grammar and vocabulary, you can be comforted by these figures: you can get by with 50 per cent accuracy in grammar and you can get by with a general vocabulary that comprises 5 per cent of the high frequency words used by native speakers.

Attending classes is the most common way that people learn foreign languages, but most learning comes from doing. You can learn French sufficiently to survive: to eat, find a hotel room, find the toilet, find the *métro*, add up the restaurant bill, and so on. This kind of learning is *primi* (from *primitif*) *Français*. You should be able to learn this type of French fairly quickly, since you are going to ignore 50 per cent of the grammar, acquire only the vocabulary you need and practice your pronunciation. *Primi Français* is functional but limited.

A step above and beyond that is mini-French, which uses articles and conjugate verbs and adds attributes. It is the French of French children who are learning their language. It contains a considerably larger vocabulary and attempts to observe the speech contours of French statements and questions instead of the hortatory, declamatory production of primi French. Thus one moves from *Pain, s'il vous plaît* to *Je voudrais du pain, s'il vous plaît*.

A tutor who is a native speaker of a foreign language may prove to be a good solution for learners who have gone beyond the practices of the classroom and want to create their own programmes. Tutors may be expensive, so you should have fairly compelling reasons for giving up the classroom for self-instruction with good tapes and texts. Tutors who are simple agreeable native speakers will probably not have sufficient experience or skill to satisfy the learner looking for alternative ways of learning.

Television, video tapes, video disks and computers offer us further the potentialities for language instruction. Any method you try will help.

Envoi (The Moral of the Story)

Learning French may not be necessary for people who want to visit for a short time in France. With the European Union now well established, the French are speaking more English. But learning French will give you a wider world of pleasure in France. And a deeper cultural understanding as well.

WORKING IN FRANCE

CHAPTER 9

'As internationalists, we have, indeed, tremendous
power, and our home-country business skills alone
are no longer sufficient in themselves.'
—Robert T. Moran, 'Cross-Cultural Contact' column
in *International Management Magazine*, July 1985

OFFICE AND BUSINESS RELATIONSHIPS
Learning to Work With the French

So far, we have talked mostly about living among the French. Now we plunge into the far more complex subject of inter-cultural relations in business: how you work with the French. If you get this wrong, it costs your company even more than your discomfort and misunderstanding.

Don't worry, all that you have learned in the previous chapters will serve you well. American authors Philip R. Harris and Robert T. Moran's wrote *Managing Cultural Differences* two decades ago and it is still the bible of cross-cultural understanding. Moran, who has lived and worked in France, encourages cultural diversity in business, both to get a better global approach towards the marketplace and to enlarge the pool of management resources.

Moran compares working internationally to fighting with two swords. At the same time as we use the personality traits that have made us successful at home: aggressiveness and competitiveness, for example, we have to learn to use a second sword of gentleness, cooperation, indirectness and commitment to relationships.

Much is being written on this subject. The European Union has made far broader demands of the French in cross-cultural understanding. Projects like EuroDisney have been fodder for many articles on cross-cultural miscommunications.

Also note that the second half of Chapter 4 defines the term 'culture shock' and describes the various stages of it for people who are coming to live and work in France. Meanwhile, here are a few important points on doing business.

Connections with your company's French branch will put you several steps ahead, when you come to France to do business. You will have the background of your old job for continuity and commitment. The local office can help you with important connections like work visas, office supplies, communication services and transportation. But even with a French office as your helping hand, don't expect to feel 'at home' in the beginning.

Hari Bedi's Five C's

Hari Bedi is an Indian expatriate working internationally. He suggests five C's in doing business internationally:

- continuity (a sense of history and tradition),
- commitment (to the growth of the organisation),
- connections (where social skills and social standing count),
- compassion (balancing scientific and political issues) and
- cultural sensitivity (a respect for other ways of doing things).

These are very essential points when doing business in France. Forget capitalism as your first priority; it is cultural sensitivity you need most.

Less emphasis will be put on your individual performance than on cooperation and flexibility. Teamwork is essential to the French. That strong spirit of competition and the drive to succeed that got you to France in the first place may not serve you so well now that you are here.

Many things, visible and invisible, are different in a French bureau: from the paper clips to the filing containers to the standard size of the paper to the way meetings are conducted.

From the instant you arrive, your language skills will be challenged. You should start now, gearing up on comprehension skills, both in language and in the silent rules of the French way of doing business. Those pleasant French associates who spoke English so well during your brief visits to France in the past now expect you to speak French.

> ### The Office Layout
> We already know French life revolves around circles of relationship, those marbles in a jar. These 'radiating networks' define a French office, and how everything is connected. The manager's desk will often be in the middle of the room with his staff surrounding him. He or she is the central figure in a hierarchy that involves many staff working as equal satellites. That manager, in turn, will answer to the PDG (*Président Directeur Général*), who is himself surrounded by a team of managers. This is a firm patriarchal structure, with the real power focused at the PDG. Don't forget your position in this layout.

Many of the office staff will turn out to be uncomfortable with English and a bit resentful towards it, because it makes their job harder. Regardless of your success and track record, you will be considered with some suspicion. You may represent the higher, central authority of the company, on whom all is blamed and to whom little is credited. Or you may just represent complications to the hierarchy everyone is already familiar with.

Shaking Hands

You will be expected to shake hands with everyone when you are introduced, remember their names and titles, and shake hands again at your departure, saying *Au revoir, Directeur Le Blanc*. You will be shaking hands again at the beginning and the end of each day, with everyone in the office. And you have sealed no deals, yet!

You must deal now with a new game of personal relationships. You must learn what motivates your new co-workers. Your affiliations and achievement orientation may be vastly different from theirs.

You may find your co-workers more concerned about job security than charge-ahead-capitalism. Time is less linear in France and its value is not measured by money alone. You will not automatically earn respect based on your professional accomplishments. As we have learned already, individuality and personality count for much among the French.

There is ambivalence towards money itself among the French. So expect to find some ambivalence in the work place. Your relationship with each member of the team will be a more important concern than controlling organisational decisions. (You probably won't have any major decisions to make anyway.) You gain trust and respect through your ability to work with the others.

Thus the very traits that had been your strengths back home may become weaknesses in France. Harris and Moran describe the rigid structure of French organisations. Authority is more centralised, most individuals in the company have less authority and so decisions are usually reached more slowly. They must come down from the top. To defend their position in the system, workers will build walls of protection, rather than take aggressive action.

Paper Cuts

If you are used to the American 8.5 x 11 inch letter standard of paper, you will find the rest of the world uses an A4 standard, which is taller and narrower by nearly an inch. Likewise, the storage of files is handled in boxes rather than file cabinets, and American paper doesn't fit into them. Nor does American paper fit into French business envelopes. Your computer will have to resize your documents for the French printers.

Several projects may be going on at once, with the same staff, and only the central authority will be capable of communicating what is really going on. You will need to carefully analyse the patterns. Listening and observing will be your essential skills.

Company Acquaintances

The French do not usually seek friendships among their business relations. There are too many of them, for one thing. And, within a French company, structured patterns of authority discourage casual, relaxed relationships.

When working in a French company, it is better to be pleasantly surprised by a co-worker's generosity and warmth than to expect it and be disappointed. Don't take it personally. That Gallic coolness is a necessity of French life. Remember the emotional burdens of friendships once they are established.

This sounds contradictory. On the one hand, office relationships are very important, but on the other hand friendships are rare. The distinction is between the levels of commitment.

Few office workers will offer the ego-building emotional support you might have enjoyed back home. Office relations are important but delicate in France. There is a constant tension between the functions of the job and the relationships defined by the job descriptions.

Although the French firmly believe in the ideal of equality, the social structure remains quite rigid. (*Remember the* grandes eçoles *we discussed in* Chapter Two: From the Celts to Rollerblades *on page 12*). Those elites schools produce most of the leaders of commerce in France. Everyone knows who the graduates are and everyone expects them to run the show. This is not the kind of democracy you knew at home.

Sending A Registered Letter

Something in writing carries more weight than a personal visit. A registered letter is binding legal proof and people feel bound to respond to it. In general, when doing business with any agency or company, it is always best to send a letter (in good French). Next most effective is to send a fax. To sort out some complicated things, of course, you must go in person. Knowing someone, or making friends with someone in the office you are dealing with will make a big difference.

Formality will be your key. Always use the *vous* form among business acquaintances and never use first names, even with your own secretaries, unless the French person suggests it. If you are unsure whether a woman is married or not, use *Madame* rather than *Mademoiselle*, as the latter also implies a spinster (an undesirable state among the family-oriented French). Use those job titles, too.

Avoid any but the most polite and patient approach to fellow workers, and be sure your business letters follow the formal French code.

That handshaking exercise we described in 'The Circular Handshake' on page 63 symbolises both the importance and the formality of relations in a French office. It gives a degree of equality among the French, but not a great degree. Everybody does it, because some gesture of equality is important. But they aren't committing much.

Though a Frenchman considers his five weeks' paid vacation sacrosanct, he will rarely take a day off without pay. He will stick to his desk, his job and his position. So should you. As a representative of the home office, you will be treated with a certain esteem. You will be expected to respond accordingly.

Trying to establish a back-slapping, hail-fellow-well-met camaraderie around the office is not going to work. Your job is to uphold your part of the web of office relationships, according to the French expectations.

Take each of your relationships at the office as unique and delicate and learn to recognise the links of communication and function so you don't accidentally strain them.

Don't try to impress people with your accomplishments or abilities. Try to direct attention away from yourself and towards an understanding of the business problem at hand, listening to all positions. Remember thesis, antithesis, synthesis.

Watch for subtle signs of class distinction in your co-workers. Respect these roles by maintaining yours. Your first goal is to learn to work with these people. Don't let someone's haughtiness put you off. The French play a class distinction game with each other all the time. Once people feel secure in their role with you, they will not feel the need for posturing. As with the waiter, your job is to help make them feel comfortable by recognising and appreciating their real job.

As you begin to understand office politics better, you will come across a system of connections called the *piston*, which is the way French describe being pushed forward in one's career by a helpful superior. This is quite popular in France, a way of seeking out the 'cream' in a group of co-workers. It may seem unjust to you, but connections count enormously in France. You will need to learn to use them too.

First Contact—The Telephone As Enemy

The French chat for hours on the phone with their friends, but they strongly resist talking to strangers, even in French. You cannot depend on the telephone as an introduction in business.

Raymonde Carroll devotes a whole chapter to this subject in her book *Cultural Misunderstandings*. When you first call an office or shop, you will often get the impression that you had better hurry up with your questions, that you are taking valuable time away from the person on the other end. They will ask for your name before they volunteer any other information or service. They may only give their first name back to you, thereby remaining safely anonymous.

The telephone pressures the person answering to make a commitment he or she may not be prepared to make. We already know the French like to think about all the options before making their first step. In business, such decisions usually come from the top.

Your call comes as an unwelcomed surprise to a lowly staff person. It distracts them from the real work at hand, their desk papers and the people around them. (Even if it is their job to answer the phone.) Such a telephone call is similar to having someone knock on your door, unannounced, but worse. At the door, you can use the peephole and see who it is. You can get an idea of that person by watching his facial expressions; you can figure him out a bit before deciding to open the door.

On the telephone, none of this important personal connection is possible. It leaves the receiver of the call in a very vulnerable position. You can start to see why the French respond so poorly to telephone calls from strangers.

For similar reasons, a French person will use the phone first to complain. It leaves him anonymous and puts the person he is calling on the defensive. So most of the calls a receptionist takes are complaints!

Rather than use the telephone to make appointments, write a formal letter. Better still send an introductory letter from a French contact. When you must use the phone, keep your requests brief and very polite.

Meetings

When a meeting is called, it will be more formally conducted than you are used to, though the appointed hour may be more flexible. Unless the home team is very international, the meetings will be conducted in French, and protocol will be strict. The top person will run the show. You may be asked to give your opinions. You may only be given instructions.

Usually, many ideas will be brought forward, though there may be no decision concluded, even though discussions run overtime. You will be judged by the coherence of your presentation, if it was asked for, and your skills at contributing to everyone's greater comprehension of the issues at hand. It will not be your job to reach a concensus.

Everyone should get the chance to voice their opinion and discussions may get far more heated than they would

On the one hand, office relationships are very important, but on the other hand, friendships are rare.

in your business meetings at home. The person chairing the meeting will usually remain passive, listening. It is his responsibility to reach a conclusion, but not necessarily at the end of the meeting.

Negotiations

According to Bob Moran, the French consider negotiation as they would a grand debate. At the conclusion of such debate, well-reasoned solutions can be found. Yet often after such a heated debate, nothing spectacular will seem to have been concluded. Sometimes, in what seems to be mid-debate, the subject may change completely, leaving one whole issue hanging.

Don't worry. Such airing of opinions is an important part of solving a problem. A great matter will take a great deal of time to consider. Don't expect everyone to agree with your opinions.

Let's break for lunch.

THE BUSINESS LUNCH

As we know from Chapter Six, lunch is a great place to establish good relations with French co-workers. Few would consider a meal without wine and this gives everyone a chance to relax and get to know each other, putting the office dynamics temporarily aside. The general rule is: no discussion of business until the cheese course (at the end, just before coffee)!

Often the subject of work will not ever be discussed. Lunch is a time for enjoying the senses and the intellect, for feeling alive. There is more to life than making money, at least in France.

Arriving at an office for a meeting just before lunch hour will not endear you to a hungry colleague or customer, nor will you find him very responsive immediately after a big lunch with wine. If you are trying to establish a good relationship with this person, suggest lunch, instead.

Taking each other out for lunch is a common goodwill gesture among business acquaintances in France. If you want to treat, state your desire to pay clearly with your invitation.

The topic should not be left to later debate.

'Ventre affamé n'a pas d'oreille.'
(A hungry stomach has no ears.)

In better restaurants, the waiter will look around the table and decide which person is supposed to pay the bill as soon as you arrive. That person will get a dollop of wine to test in before the waiter serves the rest. If you are paying, make sure you accept that dollop of wine, taste it and approve it, even if you aren't drinking any of it.

Wine with the meal is not just one of life's pleasures in France, it is expected. A glass of wine relaxes everyone and helps get the conversation going. But inebriation is totally unacceptable. It takes two hours for eight ounces of wine to work its way through your system. So unless you will be able to take a nap after lunch, don't drink more than a glass or two during the meal.

If you don't want to drink and you are not paying, you don't have to accept the first glass, but it is more gracious to do so and sip it slowly. Order a bottle of water, as well.

At table with business associates, don't be surprised if the topic turns immediately to politics and your views are solicited. Politics raise passions and inspire the intellect, just the ticket for lunch time entertainment, to the French way of thinking. Expect things to get lively.

Your opinions need not agree with anyone else's, but you better be ready to defend them, because the French love nothing better than a discussion of all aspects of the issue. As we have learned in the previous chapter, the art of conversation delights in analysis. The goal is stimulating discussion, a meaningful outlet for the intellect.

You already know the topics to avoid. Generally, you want to be sure that everyone participates and don't hog the limelight.

The French used take two-hour lunches religiously, to talk as much as to eat. While they are habituated to this noontime diversion, they are drinking less these days and taking shorter lunches so they can get back to work. It is unfortunate, as there is nothing so rich in cultural pleasures as a lengthy French midday meal, especially when you have to return to an office.

ESTABLISHING A BUSINESS IN FRANCE

Your embassy in France, or the French Chamber of Commerce and Industry (CCIP) will be able to help you in establishing a business in France. The CCIP publishes a booklet in English describing the basics of French law regarding businesses here. Ask for *How to Start a Business in France*. It gives you, in a very thorough Anglo-Saxon manner, a step-by-step approach to administrative formalities, but you should certainly consider private legal assistance, as well.

Company Structures in France:

Entreprise	This is the equivalent of a sole proprietorship in US law, and the owner's personal and business assets are both liable. A spouse may become a partner by registering as well.
SARL	A minimum of 7,500 euros and 2–50 shareholders are required for this kind of company. Shareholders' liability is limited to individual contributions.

EURL Similar to the S.A.R.L., this allows the manager to limit his liability to his individual contribution while maintaining financial control.

SNC General partnerships require no minimum capital and the partners have the status of traders, but each is jointly and separately liable for debts.

SA This is either a privately-owned or a fully public company, with a minimum of 37,000 euros capital, at least seven shareholders and no maximum. If it is fully public, the rules are more strict.

Subsidiaries, Branches and Agencies

If you want to establish a subsidiary company of one currently existing elsewhere, you also have some further choices. The subsidiaries are autonomous legal entities, economically dependent on the parent company. Their managers must obtain a *carte de commerçant étranger* or a *carte de résidence*, depending on their nationality. In some cases, they must also file a declaration of investment with the Treasury Department before registering.

Your company can also set up an agency or branch in France, for whose debts the company is totally liable. For this, you must register with the Trade Register, provide two certified copies of the company's Memorandum and Articles of Association translated into French, provide the name of the manager of the French branch as well as the birth certificate and French registration of all personnel.

A liaison office is even more informal and registration is not required, as long as you are only establishing contacts, handling publicity and collecting information in France.

Commercial and Employee requirements

If you are not French and planning to operate as a sole trader, a partner of an SNC, a manager of an SNC, SARL. or French branch, subsidiary or liaison office, or the general manager or chairman of the board of an SA, then you need either a resident's card, an EU passport or a commercial licence.

If you are not holding an EU passport, your ability to work in France is strictly controlled. If you are being assigned by your company to work in France, or you are coming to France to work for a French concern, you must get a visa before you arrive from the nearest French consulate or embassy.

For individuals seeking to live or work in France, it is essential to get good legal advice before you arrive. Everything you need to know about visas and other requirements pre-arrival can be found at the French Ministry of Foreign Affairs website (in English!). Just google 'France Visa'.

BACK AT THE HOME OFFICE

For similar reasons, your company will express little interest in the 'expertise' you've gained in working at the French branch. Normally, they will assume the French locals are the experts. You were just a go-between. You're back; the job's done. The next person assigned to Paris will have to go through all the painful learning experiences you did. Those bridges you painstakingly built between yourself and the Paris staff will be meaningless to a boss who has never needed them himself.

This opacity towards international business relations is changing, in part thanks to the European Union. Companies are starting to develop sensitivities to the invisible aspects of international relations. They are beginning to recognise that language skills are not enough. The synergy of business relations requires deep inter-cultural understanding. Increasingly, international staff, like yourself, will be called to make the different applications of company policy work abroad.

The expanded view of the world that the international worker brings to the office also makes certain local aspects of the job at home less satisfying. But such expansion is essential in international living and international relations, both in business and in politics. You are just the messenger. Expect to take a bit of heat for it, and don't despair, your message is important.

FAST FACTS
ABOUT FRANCE

CHAPTER 10

'Oou, la la!'
—Maurice Chevalier, et al.

Official Name
France

Capital
Paris

Major Cities
Paris (ten times the next largest in population), Lyon, Marseille, Lille, Toulouse and Bordeaux

Administrative Centre
Paris (the centre of everything in France)

Flag
Three equal vertical bands of blue (hoist side), white, and red; known as the 'Le drapeau tricolore' (French Tricolour)

National Anthem
La Marseilles

Time
France is one time zone, usually one hour earlier than GMT (Greenwich Mean Time) but the UK and France sometimes switch from/to daylight savings on different weekends, meaning they could be on the same time, briefly, or two hours apart.

Telephone Country Code
33

Territory
The country is divided into 100 *departements*. Ninety-six are in France proper and the island of Corsica. The four Départments d'Outre-Mer (DOM) consist of Martinique and Guadeloupe in the Caribbean, French Guiana in South America, Mayotte and l'Isle de la Reunion in the Indian Ocean, and two islands off the east coast of Canada: Saint Pierre and Miquelon.

A group of Territoires d'Outre-Mer (TOM) are also legally part of France, French Polynesia, French Southern and Antarctic Territories, New Caledonia and Wallis and Futuna Islands, as well as many small islands in the southern oceans.

All the peoples of all these outlying posts are philosophically and legally French citizens, if racially quite distinguishable.

Land Area
547,030 sq km (211,209.5 sq miles)

Highest Point
Mont Blanc in the Alps

Major Rivers
Seine, Rhone, Garonne, Loire, Rhine

Climate
Temperate

Natural Resources
Coal, iron ore, bauxite, zinc, uranium, antimony, arsenic, potash, feldspar, fluorospar, gypsum, timber, fish

Population
There are 60 million French people today. In the Paris area, there are 12 million, with two million of those inside the city proper. Almost half of the 20 to 25-year-olds live in the greater

Paris area. Many of the rest live in the other large cities. Thus the countryside's population is aging and its density quite low (101 people per sq km).

Ethnic Groups
Celtic and Latin with Teutonic, Slavic, North African, Indochinese, Basque minorities

Religion
Roman Catholic 83–88 per cent, Protestant 2 per cent, Jewish 1 per cent, Muslim 5–10 per cent, unaffiliated 4 per cent

Languages and Dialects
French 100 per cent; rapidly declining regional dialects and languages are Provencal, Breton, Alsatian, Corsican, Catalan, Basque, Flemish

Government
France has a strong centralised government, and the centre is Paris. A quarter of the work force (six million people) is in some form of civil service or another. Napolean is given much credit for establishing this 'army' of administrators. Bureaucracy rules in France. The selection process guarantees that the best minds in the country will be in the public service and 500 *grands ecoles* prepare them for the jobs. The French accept this level of interference in their lives, and the costs associated, because it works.

Administrative Divisions
22 regions; Alsace, Aquitaine, Auvergne, Basse-Normandie, Bourgogne, Bretagne, Centre, Champagne-Ardenne, Corse, Franche-Comte, Haute-Normandie, Ile-de-France, Languedoc-Roussillon, Limousin, Lorraine, Midi-Pyrenees, Nord-Pas-de-Calais, Pays de la Loire, Picardie, Poitou-Charentes, Provence-Alpes-Cote d'Azur, Rhone-Alpes
Note: metropolitan France is divided into 22 regions (including the 'territorial collectivity' of Corse or Corsica)

and is subdivided into 96 departments; see separate entries for the overseas departments (French Guiana, Guadeloupe, Martinique, Reunion) and the overseas territorial collectivities (Mayotte, Saint Pierre and Miquelon)

The Major Political Parties

UMP (Union pour un Mouvement Populaire)
Newly formed conservative coalition consisting of the former Rally for the Republic (RPR), Union for the French Democracy (UDF), and Liberal Democracy (DL) parties, led by Alain Juppé.

PS (Socialist Party)
United by François Mitterrand in 1971, it was the largest party in the National Assembly until the 1993 election. Its members include former prime ministers Michel Rocard and Lionel Jospin.

PC (Communist Party)
Only 9 per cent of the voters belong to this party now, when nearly 30 per cent of France was communist in 1946.

FN (National Front)
The right-wing organisation which is based in Marseilles, anti-immigrant and nationalistic, has become a major force on the French Riviera. Jean-Marie Le Pen is the leader.

MRG (Movement of Radicals of the Left)
This party maintains 8–12 per cent of the vote, on a par with the extreme right National Front.

Currency
The euro € became the sole currency of France on 1 January 2002.

Gross Domestic Product
US$ 28,700 (2004 est.)

Agricultural Products
Beef, cereals, dairy products, fish, potatoes, sugar beets, beef, wheat, wine grapes

Industries
Aircraft, automobiles, chemicals, electronics, food processing, machinery, metallurgy, textiles, tourism

Exports
Aircraft, beverages, chemicals, iron and steel, machinery and transportation equipment, pharmaceutical products and plastics

Imports
Aircraft, chemicals, crude oil, machinery and equipment and vehicles

Ports and Harbours
Bordeaux, Boulogne, Cherbourg, Dijon, Dunkerque, La Pallice, Le Havre, Lyon, Marseille, Mulhouse, Nantes, Paris, Rouen, Saint Nazaire, Saint Malo, Strasbourg

Airports
Charles de Gaulle and Orly serve Paris. Each major city also has an international airport.

Railways
SNCF, RER, TGV within France, as well as the IC services connecting France to the rest of Europe.

Weights and Measures
France uses the metric system.

Famous People
Clovis (AD 466–511)
A Frankish king who became a Christian and rousted the last of the Romans, uniting the country and giving it the Germanic name.

Charlemagne (AD 742–814)

A Frank who was crowned Holy Roman Emperor in AD 800. He extended his rule over northern parts of Spain and Italy as well as much of Germany. The empire collapsed after his death, but he made education compulsory though he was himself illiterate.

Louis XIV, The Sun King

He reigned from 1643–1715 and became absolute monarch. His palace at Versailles is testimony to his power. During his reign, French culture blossomed and the French language became the universal language of law and diplomacy in the Western world.

Napoleon Bonaparte (1769–1821)

A military man from Corsica who came up through the ranks to eventually become crowned emperor. He created the legal structure that still defines France today. The national civil legal system, the 'Code Napoleon', and the army of bureaucrats he organised to administer became the longest lasting contributions to his country. He died in exile in the southern Atlantic Ocean.

Charles de Gaulle (1900–1970)

He led the free French from England during World War II and brought France back to prosperity after the war. While he said no one could rule a country with 265 cheeses, he did so very well, thanks to a strong central government.

Jacques Chirac

Current President of France under the Fifth Republic established by De Gaulle. An enarque, graduate of the elite school for administrator established by De Gaulle, Chirac has led his country into the European Union.

Simone de Beauvoir

From a group of writers of French-language literature, including Andre Malraux, Albert Camus and Jean Paul

Sartre who struggled with human suffering and identity in the middle of the 20th century. Her book, *The Second Sex* is considered seminal in the Women's Liberation Movement.

Asterix, Cartoon character, now almost 50 years old

This little Gaul set in the time of the Romans, created by Albert Uderzo and Rene Goscinny, mocks and celebrates many characteristics of the French. Cartoons (*bande-dessinée*) are enjoyed in France and celebrated each year at a festival in Angouleme.

Edith Piaf and the other French jazz singers of the mid-20th century, including Geroges Brassens, Jacques Brel and Yves Montand. Their voices are still heard everywhere in France and throughout the world.

Claude Debussy and Maurice Ravel

Fathers of modern music in the classical tradition. Both lived into the first decades of the 20th century.

Brothers Louis and Auguste Lumiere

They invented cinema in 1895. The Cannes Film Festival that was started in 1946 awards the highest honours in international film today. Though the French film industry is subsidised by the state, the productions are brilliant.

Auguste Rodin (1840–1917)

Was perhaps France's most famous sculptor. His museum is next to the Invalides in Paris, where famous works such as 'The Thinker' and 'The Kiss' are found.

Artists of Impressionism

Impressionism was born in France, inspiring famous artists such as Claude Monet, Pierre-Auguste Renior, Edgar Degas, Paul Cezanne, Henry Rousseau, Henri Matisse, George Braque and Pablo Picasso (A Spaniard who lived most of his life in France).

Gustave Eiffel
The French engineer who designed the tower bearing his name. Built in 1889 and bitterly contested at that time, it is perhaps the most enduring symbol of all things French.

Acronyms

AOC (Appelation d'Origine Contrôlée)
Agricultural, alcoholic or dairy products which meet specific standards of production are labelled thus, indicating highest quality

EDF (Électricité de France)
French public electricity providers

GDF (Gaz de France)
French public gas providers

PACS (Pacte Civil de Solidarité)
New civil solidarity agreement allowing unmarried couples, both gay and straight, to enjoy the same privileges as married couples

RER (Réseau Express Régional)
Trains passing under Paris, linking to the *métro* but also serving the surrounding suburban communities

RATP (Régie Autonome des Transports Parisians)
The public transportation system of Paris

SAMU (Service d'Aide Médicale d'Urgence)
Public ambulance and emergency medical services

SNCF (Société Nationale des Chemins de Fer Français)
French railway system

TGV (Train à Grande Vitesse)
The high speed long-distance trains of France

Places of Interest

All of France is of great interest but here are just a few of the most famous.

The Eiffel Tower

This symbol of France, is a 100-year-old engineering brainstorm of a single Frenchman. Elevators powered by the Seine River take visitors to the top view deck, and restaurant. You can also walk up!

The Arc de Triomphe

This was built by Napoleon and is part of the group of architectural wonders of the world. The corridor going from the Louvre Palace (now a museum) all the way out to the new Arch at La Defense in the suburbs. It is accessible now only by underground passageway as 10 lanes of traffic circle it anti-clockwise day and night. You can climb to the top for another grand view of the City of Light.

The Louvre

The palace of royalty for centuries, is now one of the world's largest museums. Long lines of waiting visitors wrap around the building during the tourist season. Best to buy a 'Paris Visite' card which will give you access to this and many other tourist sites of Paris without waiting in line for a ticket. The card will also get you on all public transportation.

Notre Dame Cathedral

Famous for its flying buttresses and stained glass windows, this was built on as island in the middle of the Seine, in the middle of Paris. Try to go when they are giving a music recital.

Chartres Cathedral

Less than an hour away by train, this cathedral is the centre piece of a medieval town. It elegantly illustrates the 'star' pattern of France's countryside. The Cathedral sits upon a hill, visible from roads coming from all directions, and

The famous Eiffel Tower.

towers above the town, which has been beautifully protected from modernisation.

Marseilles

Of the many port cities around France, this one is a surprise. One expects the ugly modern elements of container shipping (which exist) but the old city has been preserved and repaired, and the old harbour is filled with pleasure and working boats. It hasn't got the sexy allure of Cannes or St Tropez, but is a beautiful honest working city, founded by the Greeks centuries before Christ. You can get there in three hours on the TGV from Paris.

Jardin de Luxembourg.
On the left bank, with the Senate at one side, this is a formal French garden, once for royalty, now preserved for the public to enjoy. As with most of the parks in France, it closes at sundown. And please don't walk on the grass.

La Villette
The most modern museum in France, dedicated to the latest technology and the computer arts. You can get there by canal barge, one of the oldest means of transportation in Europe.

CULTURE QUIZ

SITUATION 1

An evening at a good French restaurant is planned with friends who are visiting Paris for the first time. You've made reservations and arrive a bit late to find the *maître d'* cool and the waiters unfriendly. Your guests complain that French people are rude. Do you:

Ⓐ Agree with your friends and concede that this is just another example, making it a good evening in spite of the unfriendliness by laughing with your friends at the supercilious attitude of the staff?

Ⓑ Ignore your friends' comment and apologise for being late and strive all evening to make up for it to the restaurant staff?

Ⓒ Interpret the attitude at the restaurant as normal and brush off your friends' comments?

Ⓓ Strive to explain to your friends about the Paris waiter's rudeness game and show him how to play it, in return?

Ⓔ Attempt through your serious interest in the wine and cuisine to win over the waiters and prove your friends wrong?

Comments

This situation comes up so many times in Paris, it should be in every guidebook. French waiters are professionals; they take their work seriously and with pride. By recognising them as professionals, you can avoid the emotional reaction of feeling rejected by their coolness, and teach your compatriots to adopt the French attitude towards food. So, **Ⓔ** is the most productive. Though you can still enjoy your evening with your friends by ignoring the situation, it in turn makes you appear rude to the restaurant staff and reconfirms their view that foreigners don't appreciate French cuisine or behave properly in public.

SITUATION 2

You've just moved into your apartment and you need to order telephone service/plumbing repairs/electrical service. Do you:

Ⓐ Call the company and try to make arrangements over the telephone?

Ⓑ Visit your nearest Telecom office, plumber or EDF shop and ask them for the service you need, in person?

Ⓒ Contact the *gardienne* or concierge in your building and ask them to handle the job for you, expecting to pay a handsome tip?

Ⓓ Ask your secretary at work to handle these details?

Comments

In France, people tend to do their own chores, and there is little crossover between personal and private life. Your secretary will not expect to have such private matters in her hands. Although the *gardienne* in your building could help you with some details of private life, you will find things happen most expediently when you go, in person, to the office or service company you require. It is usually more difficult to get anything like services, train reservations and specific information accomplished over the telephone. Projects such as the telephone service installation will take some time, standing in lines, filling out forms and showing identification. Take along all your documents and have all your questions ready in advance. Remember, only your specific questions will be answered and few helpful suggestions will be volunteered. Treat the person helping you as you would treat a stranger giving requested assistance. Expect less than enthusiastic response to your dilemma. Take some reading material, to occupy your time while waiting. Be patient. The best option is **Ⓑ**.

SITUATION 3

You have just arrived at the company offices where you will be working in Paris. You have already met most of your fellow workers on previous visits. A group at the office is going to lunch and invite you to join them, but once at the restaurant the conversation turns to politics, and a roaring argument develops, in French. Your reaction is:

Ⓐ To sit in shock, unable to eat, fearing physical violence will erupt at any moment.

Ⓑ Realise that your new French friends have turned their back on you, speaking quickly in French to one another without regard for your limited language skills. Assume you are an outsider and expected to sit quietly by while they discuss the details of their own political situation.

Ⓒ Vow to improve your language skills so that you can participate, and follow the conversation closely.

Ⓓ Make your comments, if you understand the gist of the conversation, even if you can only express yourself in English, when there is a lull in the conversation and you see a chance to jump in without interrupting.

Ⓔ Scold the group for being far too heated on the subject of politics and try to turn the conversation back to English and to matters of business that are on your mind.

Comments

Option **Ⓓ**. Many French people love to discuss and debate, especially on the subject of politics. Debate, itself, is an art form, in France, and their English skills may not be sufficient for such parrying. So resign yourself to French, during the lunch hour, often to heated debates, especially on the subject of politics. Your growing skills in the language, and growing knowledge of French politics will make these experiences more interesting. They are a vital part of living in France.

SITUATION 4

You are invited to dinner with French acquaintances. It starts at 8:00 pm and you arrive early to an elegant apartment, with a bottle of white wine which needs chilling. You offer to put the bottle in the refrigerator and ask where the kitchen is. Your hostess takes the wine, leads you to the living room, instead and keeps you there until dinner is served in the dining room. After the meal, you depart the same way you came in, feeling you've been treated too much as a stranger and not enough as a friend. You wanted to see the whole apartment! Do you:

Ⓐ Assume that you have been given the 'cold shoulder' and refuse their next invitation as insincere?

Ⓑ Confront your acquaintances and ask them what you did 'wrong', but find that they don't seem to understand your question?

Ⓒ Feel distanced from these people but reciprocate your hosts' efforts, nonetheless, with a dinner at your favourite restaurant. In that environment, they appear to be more open and friendly.

Ⓓ Return to your hosts' home and expect, this time, to be entertained only in the living room and dining room, recognising that your presence in the house is already a display of intimacy, even if the rest of the house is off limits.

Ⓔ Confront your hosts in the first place and ask to see the house when you first arrive.

Comments

The French do not have a habit of 'showing off' their house to first-time guests. It would be considered boastful as well as too intimate. Plus they probably haven't got the rest of the house looking as perfect as the part they intend for you to enjoy. So if you really want to see the house, ask in advance of your arrival, to give them time to prepare it for you properly. Otherwise, if you are not invited to take a look around it, don't ask yourself into any room that is not shown to you (except of course the toilet, which you can ask for!). Accept this modesty and don't mistake it for haughtiness.

SITUATION 5

You are on the street looking for a certain gourmet food shop. Your time is short and you've left the address at home. Which of the following people do you ask for help:

A A policeman ambling down the street?

B A businessman with a briefcase briskly walking the same way?

C An older woman in black bent over and moving slowly towards the *métro*?

D A fashionable, well-dressed woman of middle age waiting for the light?

Comments

Choosing the person from whom you ask directions in France is very important, when seeking a good answer. Unless your question involves traffic law, don't seek the help of a policeman, or anyone else in uniform. They do not consider it their job to direct either locals or foreigners, and they often do not speak English, anyway. The same goes for the *métro* ticket seller. Giving directions is not part of his or her job. A person with a brisk walk may well be in a hurry, best not to interrupt him or her, as a proper explanation may take time and patience this isn't currently able to give. Finally, an older woman in black is probably from the countryside and may not know the area well, plus she certainly wouldn't be frequenting gourmet food stores. It's best to choose the person most likely to frequent the shop and least preoccupied with other duties.

SITUATION 6

You are included in your first business meeting at work. Your boss acts as chairperson and he requests progress reports on a specific project from various members of your teams dealing with different aspects of the job. To your surprise, as each person's turn comes, he or she seems full of complaints and problems to report, often turning blame for the situation on your boss. Your turn comes. Do you:

A Take the same stand, presenting your situation as too difficult and demanding help from your boss?

B Pass, leaving your report unsaid?

⊙ Give the report you had planned to give, outlining the current situation but without any criticism or complaint?

⊙ Turn to other members of the group whom you feel have unfairly criticised the boss and explain your opinion?

⊙ Assume that your boss is just about to be fired and you'll be looking for another job tomorrow?

Comments

Meetings in France have a function similar to luncheon discussions. Members participating are expected to be critical and discriminating in their observations. Although they may appear to be putting blame on the chairman's head, such comments are more an opportunity for the speaker to exhibit his command and skill in his job. The chairman will not take honest criticism personally, but he will listen critically, as all others in the room are expected to do. So, it will not be your job to defend your boss. He does not feel threatened. It will be your job, however, to sharpen up your report to convey your own skills at discerning both negative and positive aspects of your particular situation. A sweetened version of the facts will not impress the boss with your skills. It may be taken as a false compliment. Better to prepare a sharp, observant report in advance.

SITUATION 7

You have established certain shops in your neighbourhood as your regular stops. One day, when you are in a hurry with a long shopping list, the lady who sells you cheeses begins a long explanation of the day's specials and then begins a story about a pickpocket who was apprehended by an angry victim on the street corner the previous day. You can see the story is going to take some time and you don't want to be held up indefinitely. Do you:

⊙ Interrupt the speaker, explain that you are in a hurry, and ask for your bill?

⊙ Let her finish her story and then express regret, followed immediately by "How much do I owe you?"

C Console the lady about the growing violence on the streets and confirm that active victims get better results than the police force, then say you will return for your packages later?

Comments

Relationships, both in business and personal life, are critical in France and being in a hurry is hardly considered sufficient grounds for denying your acquaintances the chance to express their concerns and convey exciting neighbourhood gossip. People you do business with regularly, especially those shopkeepers in your neighbourhood who recognise you as a regular, will make a special effort with you, as a valued customer. Such conversation is one of the ways they establish that intimacy and give special treatment. By brushing them aside, you destroy the delicate bridge of friendship that they are building. However, we all get in a hurry at times, so by apologising for your hurry and making a special effort with that shopkeeper the next time you are buying, you can avoid damage to the relationship.

DO'S AND DON'TS

DO'S

- Do say *Bonjour, Madame* etc. at the start, *Merci, Madame* etc. when appropriate and *Au revoir, Madame* etc. at the end to any person with whom you make contact working in a shop or on the street. This includes everyone from the greengrocer in the *marché* to the check-out girl at the *supermarché* to the postman.
- Do respond to the comments of the shopkeepers and expect a conversation with them, even a lengthy one, before you ask for what you came to buy.
- Do use *Madame, Monsieur* and *Mademoiselle* when saying hello and goodbye to colleagues and professional acquaintances, along with a handshake to each.
- Do respect the privacy of your neighbours. After saying *Bonjour, Madame* etc., remember silence preserves.
- Do dress your best and hold yourself as if you are proud of who and what you are.
- Do speak just loudly enough to be heard and never enough to disturb other people.
- Do hold the door open for the person behind you at all times.
- Do try to respond to someone's request for directions, or stay with them until someone else can be stopped and asked for help.
- Do ask for information and assistance from any public person as you would ask for a favour from a kind stranger. Never assume it is their job, even if it is!
- Don't touch a member of the opposite gender in public.
- Do speak softly in any public situation. As a tourist, you will sometimes find yourself seated in a restaurant room full of other noisy tourists. Then you will see why the French don't want to sit with you.
- Do feel free to discuss politics and study up on your understanding of French politics so you can be part of the conversation.

- Do return a compliment or positive comment with an expression of appreciation and respect for that person's judgement. "Oh, do you think so?" asked honestly, is your best response. Don't deny a compliment. Assume it is given in sincerity and accept it with sincerity.

- Do watch carefully, in conversation, for signs of boredom, or the desire of your listener to speak. Be ready to relinquish the floor, or change topics, at any time.

- Do expect serious and heated discussions in business meetings and dinner conversations, but don't take criticism and differing opinions personally.

- Do remember things work from the top down in French bureaucracy and be patient while a solution is found to your problem.

- Do learn as much French as possible before you arrive, and use it, even if you are not sure of your pronunciation, grammar and vocabulary. Everyone will appreciate it and help you along...even though they may wince a bit.

DON'TS

- Don't respond to comments or solicitations from strangers on the street, including 'the look' (direct eye contact with you), unless they are asking for your help.

- Don't make eye contact with strangers you don't want to engage in conversation.

- Don't walk down the street smiling at everything. In such a beautiful city, this is hard, but people will assume you are mentally feeble and possibly dangerous.

- Don't strike up conversations with strangers of the opposite sex, unless it is to give or get directions, or you are interested in getting to know them.

- Don't use first names unless the person also knows and uses your first name and is your age or younger. If they are your senior in age, use their family name until they ask you to use their first name.

- Don't ask about a person's family or a person's age unless you are on intimate terms or they have asked you similar questions, already.

- Don't ever ask what someone does for a living. It is better to discuss food than money.
- Don't make a compliment just to be polite, but do comment on things that please you.
- Don't open a closed door without knocking first. But don't wait long for a reply before entering. A knock warns that 'I'm coming in' in France.
- Don't follow your host around his house. Stay where you have been put until invited to come elsewhere. Especially stay out of the kitchen and don't even pour yourself a drink, unless invited to do so.
- Don't rush to eat your food as soon as it is put in front of you. Stop to admire the presentation and make comments on that and the experience as you slowly savour your meal
- In a restaurant, don't call out '*Garçon*', snap your fingers or clap your hands for service. The French don't respond favourably to such treatment. (Would you?)
- Don't expect a smoke-free environment. In spite of an active anti-smoking campaign, you will also find people smoking in restaurants, especially at the end of their meal. You can ask for a 'no smoking' section but as restaurants are small and not perfectly ventilated, your best bet is to sit outside if the weather allows, or by the door.
- Don't bring your own wine to a restaurant. If nothing on their wine list pleases you, go somewhere else.
- Don't ask for a 'doggy bag' as French food is meant to be eaten as soon as it is prepared. (Dogs, though, are usually welcome.)

GLOSSARY

The most common stumbling block to making oneself
understood in another language is pronunciation. Listen
carefully and try to imitate the people around you. Try to
speak with the local accent, even if you feel self-conscious
or foolish.

Generally, when we aren't completely confident in our
speaking abilities, we tend to emphasise our own peculiar
way of pronouncing words in order to maintain an element
of familiarity in a situation where everything else is strange
and foreign. This may make you feel more comfortable, but
it won't help others understand you.

Think of yourself as an actor or actress playing a role.
It is a good way to surmount these inhibitions. France is a
theatre of pleasures. Acting like you are part of the show is
a good way for both you and the person with whom you are
speaking to have some fun!

FRENCH BASICS

Bonjour; Salut	Hello
Parlez-vous anglais?	Do you speak English?
Oui	Yes
Non	No
Au Revoir; Salut	Goodbye
S'il vous plaît; S'il te plaît	Please
Excusez-moi; Pardon	Excuse me
Merci	Thank you
Je vous en prie; Je t'en prie	You're welcome
D'accord	OK; I see
Je ne comprend pas	I don't understand
Est-ce que vous pouvez parler plus lentement?	Could you speak more slowly?
Je ne sais pas	I don't know

Comment dit-on ça en français?	How do you say this in French?
Comment vous appellez-vous?	What's your name?
Je m'appelle...	My name is....
Je viens de(s)...	I come from...
Comment-allez vous? Ça va?	How are you?
Très bien, merci!	Great, thanks!
Ça va, et vous?	I'm doing OK, and you?
Ah bon?	Oh really?
Bien sûr	Of course.
Comme vous voulez; comme tu veux	As you please; as you like.
Où?	Where?
Quand?	When?
Qui?	Why?
Pourquoi?	Who?
Comment?	How?
Combien?	How many; how much?

USEFUL WORDS AND PHRASES

L'addition (f)	the bill
Un apéritif (m)	before dinner cocktail
arrondissement (m)	district (of which there are 20 in Paris)
Assemblée Nationale (f)	the French parliament
baguette (f)	name of a traditional long, thin Parisian bread
le bar (m)	small café
bar à vin (m)	wine bar
bibliothèque (f)	library
bien élevé	well brought up
billet (m)	ticket

boucherie (f)	butcher shop
boulangerie (f)	bakery
brasserie (f)	large café serving food throughout the day
café Américain (m)	watered down espresso
café au lait (m)	espresso with milk
café crème (m)	espresso with cream
café noir; un express (m)	shot of espresso
carafe d'eau (f)	a carafe of tap water served with meals in a restaurant
un carnet (m)	discounted book of ten *métro* or bus tickets
carrefour (m)	intersection; also name of giant supermarket chain
carte bleu (CB) (f)	credit/debit card
carte de résident (f)	residence permit valid for ten years
carte de séjour (f)	residence permit valid for one year
carte d'orange (f)	monthly public transportation pass valid in Paris
caution (f)	security deposit
chambre (f)	room
charcuterie (f)	deli; specialised deli meats such as *pâté* or *saucisson*
château (m)	castle, mansion
chaud(e) (mf)	hot
coiffeur (m)	hairdresser
commissariat de police (m)	police station
concierge (mf)	door keeper; caretaker
cuisine (f)	kitchen
département (m)	county

digestif (m)	after dinner liqueur
distributeur automatique de billets (m)	ATM machine; see also *point d'argent*
douche (f)	shower
eau (f)	water
église (f)	church
Énarque (m)	graduate of the ENA, top political university in France
enguelade (f)	quarrel
entrée (f)	first course; entrance
épicerie (f)	corner store
escalier (m)	stairway
étage (m)	floor, storey
étranger (m)	foreigner
femme (f)	woman
foie gras (m)	specially prepared goose liver
fonctionnaire (m)	civil service employee
froid(e) (mf)	cold
fromagerie (f)	shop selling cheese
gardien(ne) (mf)	door keeper; caretaker
gare (f)	railway station
grand magasin (m)	department store
grandes écoles (f)	most prestigious schools in the French university system
grève (m)	a demonstration or strike
homme (m)	man
hôtel (m)	aristocratic town house; hotel
hôtel de ville (m)	city hall
jardin (m)	garden

journal (m)	newspaper
kiosque (m)	news stand
librarie (m)	bookstore
location (f)	rental
mairie (f)	town hall
marché (m)	market
métro (m)	subway
Minitel (m)	'online' computer system available to France Telecom subscribers
musée (m)	museum
pain (m)	bread
pâté (m)	pork or duck based meat spread
pâtisserie (f)	shop selling pastries and cakes
place (f)	square
point d'argent (m)	ATM machine
poissonnerie (f)	shop selling fresh seafood
pont (m)	bridge
porte (f)	door
salle de bain (f)	washroom
salon de thé (m)	teahouse; upscale version of a café
sens unique (m)	one way street
tabac (m)	shop selling cigarettes, phonecards, stamps, etc. toilets
vache (f)	cow (popular animal appearing in many endearing French expressions)

vin (f)	wine
zinc (m)	the bar, where one stands in a café
toilettes (f) pl.	toilets

SHOPPING

Attention!	Careful!
Entrée	Entrance
Sortie	Exit
Ouvert	Open
Ferme	Closed
Poussez	Push
Tirez	Pull
Issue de Secours	Emergency Exit
Entrée Interdit	Do Not Enter
HS/En Panne	Out of Order
Défense de Fumer	No Smoking
Renseignements	Information
Correspondance	Transfer (métro)
Soldes	Sale

RESOURCE GUIDE

EMERGENCY NUMBERS

In an emergency contact the following numbers:

Fire: 18
Ambulance (SAMU): 15
Police: 17
SOS Medecins (in English)
(an organisation which provides 24-hour house calls.)
Tel: (01) 4723-8080
Crisis Hotline (in English)
Tel: (01) 4723-8080

ENGLISH SPEAKING HOSPITALS, DOCTORS AND PHARMACIES

Hospitals

In addition to many excellent French services, there are several hospitals catering to English speakers in Paris:

American Hospital of Paris
63 blvd Victor-Hugo; 92200 Neuilly
Tel: (01) 4641-2525
Will accept Medicaid and most American insurance policies. However, it is more expensive than other local hospitals.

Hertford British Hospital
3, rue Barbès; 92300 Levallois-Perret
Tel: (01) 4639-2222
Specialises in maternity care.

Doctors

The Australian, British, Canadian, and US embassies, as well as the American Hospital, have listings of registered English-speaking doctors and dentists within France.

Pharmacies

Most medicine in France requires a prescription. Several pharmacies serving English speakers can be found in Paris:

British and American Pharmacy
1, rue Auber; 75009 Paris
Tel: (01) 4742-4940

La Pharmacie Anglaise
62, ave des Champs-Élysées; 75008 Paris
Tel: (01) 4359-2252

Pharmacie Anglo-Américain
6, rue de Castiglione, 75001 Paris
Tel: (01) 4260-7296

For emergency dental care contact:
American Hospital of Paris (listed above)

Hôpital Hôtel Dieu
1, place du Parvis-Notre-Dame; 75004 Paris
Tel: (01) 4234-8234

SOS Dentaire
87, blvd du Port Royal; 75013 Paris
Tel: (01) 4337-5100

FACILITIES FOR THE DISABLED

In general, France does not have a lot of resources for those who are disabled. To find out more about facilities in your area, ask for information at the local town or city hall (*la mairie*). Alternatively, there are also several organisations listed below which you can go to for information.

Comité National Français Liaison Réadaptation Handicapés
236 bis, rue Tolbiac, 75013 Paris
Tel: (01) 5380-6666

FAVA (Franco-American Volunteer Association for the Mentally Retarded)
24, rue d'Alsace-Lorraine, 75019 Paris
Tel: (01) 4245-1791

RATP Voyages Accompagnés
21, blvd Bourdon, 75004 Paris
Tel: (01) 4959-9600
Free door-to-door service.

TRANSPORT AND COMMUNICATIONS

Telephone services:	14
French directory assistance:	12
International directory assistance:	003312 + country code
Minitel directory information:	3611
Phone problems:	1013

INTERNATIONAL TELEPHONE CALLS

International calling cards are available wherever local Telecartes are sold. They generally offer good rates for calling overseas. There are also heavily discounted calling cards available for sale in certain stores in the 13*eme*, 18*eme* and 19*eme*. If you already have a calling card plan via your telephone company in your home country, you can use the access numbers listed below:

AT&T:	(08) 0099-0011
Australia Optus:	(08) 0099-2061
Australia Telstra:	(08) 0099-0061
British Telecom:	(08) 0099-0044
Canada Direct:	(08) 0099-0016
MCI:	(08) 0099-0019
Sprint:	(08) 0099-0087

ACCESSING THE INTERNET

Both AOL and Compuserve are international Internet Service Providers (ISPs) that have local access numbers in Paris. If you don't have an account with either of these companies, there are plenty of French *fournisseurs d'accès* (providers) to choose from. Here are several of the more widely used ones at the time of publication:

Club Internet
http://www.club-internet.com; tel: (01) 5545-4500

Easynet France
http://www.easynet.fr; tel: (08) 1125-7000

Free
http://www.free.fr
A free ISP which is quite popular.

Wanadoo
http://www.wanadoo.fr; tel: (08) 0163-3434
Wanadoo is the ISP offered through France Télécom.

Cybercafé

If you don't have access to the Web, you will might want to stop in at a cybercafé occasionally. In addition to Internet access, coffee and tea, some cybercafés offer word processing, scanning and printing services.

- **Baguenaude Café**
  30, rue de la Grande-Truanderie, 1er
  Tel: (01) 4026-2774
- **Café Orbital**
  13, rue de Medicis, 6eme
  Tel: (01) 4325-7677
- **Clicktown**
  15, rue du Rome, 8eme
  Website: http://www.clicktown.com
- **Cyber Cube**
  12, rue Daval, 11eme
  Tel: (01) 4929-6767 (main branch)
  Website: http://www.cybercube.com
  Has four locations in Paris.
- **Easyeverything**
  31–37, blvd de Sebastopol, 1er
  Tel: (01) 4586-0877
  Has branches in over 15 cities.
- **Web Bar**
  32, rue de Picardie, 3eme

Tel: (01) 4272-6655

Free Internet services can also be found at the Centre George Pompidou, the Vidéothèque de Paris, and on avenue de Friedland near the Charles-de-Gaulle-Étoile. Be prepared to wait in line.

CULTURAL CENTRES AND CLASSES IN FRANCE

No matter what your native culture, you are going to need help in France and most sources for assistance here are open to everyone who speaks English. There are hundreds of them. Below we include a list of primary resources. Google for more.

Cultural Resources in English, French and Asian Languages

Alliance Française
101 blvd Raspail, 75006 Paris (M: Raspail)
Tel: (01) 4544-3828

The American Chamber of Commerce
156 bd Haussmann
Tel:(01) 5643-4567
Various services for members; also library. Open Tuesday to Thursday from 10:00 am to 12:30 pm for non-members and Minitel services available at CECOM on 3617 for the public.

The American Church in Paris
65 Quai D'Orsay, 75007 Paris (M: Invalides)
Tel: (01) 4062-0500
Many programs and publications in addition to ecumenical religious services. Publishes *The Free Voice* monthly newspaper in English for the Paris community.

The American Cathedral (Episcopal)
23 ave George V, 75008 Paris
Tel: (01) 5323-8400

American Embassy
2 rue St. Florentin, 75001 Paris
Tel: (01) 4312-2222
Website: www.amb-usa.fr

American Express
11 rue Scribe, 75009 Paris (M: Opera)
Tel: (01) 4714-5000

The American Library in Paris
10, rue du Général Camou, 75007 Paris
Tel: (01) 5359-1261
Open Tuesday–Saturday, 10:00 am–7:00 pm;
Website: www.americanlibraryinparis.org

The American University of Paris
31 ave Bosquet, 75007 Paris
Tel: (01) 4062-0600
Website: www.aup.edu

The Association of American Wives of Europeans
34 ave de New York, 75116 Paris
Tel: (01) 4070-1180;
Website: www.aaweparis.org
Programmes for women living in France plus two excellent
resources—Guide to Education and Living in France: Job
Hunting, Divorce, Retirement, Wills & Inheritance.

Association Culturelle Franco-Japonaise
8-12 rue Bertin Poirée, 75001 Paris
Tel: (01) 4476-0606

Association France-Etats-Unis
9, blvd Suchet, 75016 Paris
Tel: (01) 4527-8086

Australian Embassy
4 rue Jean-Rey, 75015 Paris

Tel: (01) 4059-3300;
Website: www.austgov.fr

Brentano's (English language bookstore)
37, avenue de l'Opéra, 75008 Paris (M: Opera)
Tel: (01) 4261-5250

British and Commonwealth Women's Association
8 rue de Belloy, 75116 Paris
Tel: (01) 4720-5091

The British Council
9 rue de Constantine, 75007 Paris
Tel: (01) 4955-7300; fax: (01) 4705-7702
On Minitel at 3615

British Embassy
35 rue du Faubourg St. Honoré, 75008 Paris
Tel: (01) 4451-3100
Website: www.amb-grandebretagne.fr

The British Institute in Paris
11 rue Constantine, 75007 Paris
Tel: (01) 4411-7373
Website: www.bip.lon.ac.uk

Canadian Embassy
35 ave Montaigne, 75008 Paris; tel: (01) 4443-2900;
Website: www.amb-canada.fr

CAPEC (Centre Asiatique pour la Promotion Economique et Commercial)
75 ave Marceau
Tel: (01) 4563-3354

Centre Culturel Chinois
78 rue Dunois, 75116 Paris
Tel: (01) 5689-8100

Centre Culturel Coréen
2 ave d'Iéna, 75016 Paris
Tel: (01) 4720-8386

Centre Culturel Franlasie
44 rue René Boulanger, 75010 Paris
Tel: (01) 4238-3788

Commission Franco-Américaine d'Echanges Universitaires
9 rue Chardin, 75016 Paris
Tel: (01) 4414-5360

France USA Contacts (FUSAC)
26 rue Bénard, 75014 Paris
Tel: (01) 5653-5454
Monthly publication for English-speaking people in France. Available from WICE, the American Church and other outlets.

Galignani (English language bookstore)
224 rue de Rivoli, 75001 Paris
Tel: (01) 4260-7607

Indian Embassy
15 rue Alfred-Dehodencq, 75016 Paris
Tel: (01) 4050-7070

Indonesian Embassy
49 rue Cortambert, 75016 Paris
Tel: (01) 4503-0760

Irish Embassy
4 rue Rude, 75116 Paris
Tel: (01) 4417-6700

Japanese Embassy
7 ave Hoche, 75008 Paris
Tel: (01) 4888-6200

Korean Cultural Centre
2 av d'Iena, 75016 Paris
Tel: (01) 4720-8386

L'Astrolabe (maps store)
46, rue de Provence, 75009 Paris
Tel: (01) 4285-4295

Malaysian Embassy
32 rue Spontini, 75016 Paris
Tel: (01) 4553-1185

New Zealand Embassy
7 ter rue L. deVinci, 75116 Paris
Tel: (01) 4501-4343; fax: (01) 4501-4344

Pakistan Embassy
18 rue Lord-Byron, 75008 Paris
Tel: (01) 4562-2332

Paris Notes, The Newsletter for People Who Love Paris
P.O. Box 15818, North Hollywood, CA 91615
Tel: (1-800) 677-9660;
Website: www.parisnotes.com

People's Republic of China Embassy
11 ave George V, 75016 Paris
Tel: (01) 4723-3445

Philippine Embassy
4 ham Boulainvilliers, 75116 Paris
Tel: (01) 4414-5700; fax: (01) 4647-5600

St. Michael's Church (Anglican)
5 rue d'Aguesseau, 75008 Paris
Tel: (01) 4742-7088

Shakespeare & Co. Book Store
37 rue de la Bucherie, 75005 Paris (M: St. Michel)
Tel: (01) 4326-9650

Singapore Embassy
12 ave Square Foch, 75116 Paris
Tel: (01) 4500-3361

South Korean Embassy
125 rue de Grenelle, 75007 Paris
Tel: (01) 4753-0101; fax: (01) 4753-7149

Sri Lankan Embassy
16 rue Spontini, 75016 Paris
Tel: (01) 5573-3131

Taiwan Embassy—ASPECT
78 rue Université, 75007 Paris
Tel: (01) 4439-8830
Website: www.roc-taiwan-fr.com

Thailand Embassy
8 rue Greuze, 75116 Paris
Tel: (01) 4704-3222

Vietnam Embassy (Cultural Services)
62 rue Boileau, 75116 Paris
Tel: (01) 4414-6400

The Village Voice Bookstore
6 rue Princesse, 75006 Paris (M: Mabillon)
Tel: (01) 4633-3647

W.H. Smith (English language bookstore)
248 rue de Rivoli, 75002 Paris
Tel: (01) 4477-8899

Women's Institute for Continuing Education (WICE)
20 blvd Montparnasse, 75015 Paris (M: Duroc)

Tel: (01) 4566-7550
Website: www.wice-paris.org
Part of the American University in Paris, the WICE conducts courses and programmes for the English-speaking; also an excellent guide to health services in France. Open Monday–Friday from 9:00 am–5:00 pm.

French Language Schools

Living in Paris is the ideal time to study the language. Schools abound and vary in price, class size, teaching method, and elective classes offered. So do a bit of research. Listed below are some of the more popular schools. You can look through the English language publications for information on other options, including language exchanges or private tutors.

- **Alliance Française**
  Main branch at: 101, blvd Raspail; 75270 Paris (*6eme*)
  Tel: (01) 4284-9000; email: info@alliancefr.org
  Website: http://www.alliancefr.org;
  Alliance Française can be found in many cities throughout France. They generally have decent teachers and a fair price, although the class size (22 max.) can be intimidating for some. The resource library, language lab and cultural events are among the many perks.
- **Berlitz**
  Main branch at: 15, rue Louis le Grand; 75002 Paris
  Tel: (01) 4266-6815
  Website: http://www.berlitz.com
  Berlitz has 16 schools located in France, six of which are scattered throughout Paris. They teach languages 'instinctively' in small groups or individual classes. More expensive than other schools, it's good for businessmen or women who would like to learn the language quickly. They also offer translation services.
- **Cours de Civilization Française de la Sorbonne**
  47, rue des Écoles; 75005 Paris
  Tel: (01) 4046-2211
  Website: http://www.fle.fr/sorbonne/

Probably the most rigorous language classes offered in Paris. This school uses a traditional teaching method with an emphasis on written texts and history of literature, as well as regular tests on grammar and vocabulary. Class size is generally between 15 and 25.

- **Institut Catholique de Paris**
  21, rue d'Assas; 75006 Paris
  Tel: (01) 4222-4180; email: sic@icp.fr; http://www.icp.fr
  The Institut Catholique receives high marks from its students. The focus is on both written and oral French, and the teachers often include interesting cultural anecdotes in the learning process.

- **Institut de Langue Française**
  3, ave Bertie Albrecht; 75008 Paris
  Tel: (01) 4563-2400; email: ILF@inst-langue-fr.com;
  Website: http://www.inst-langue-fr.com
  Medium size classes (max. 15) for all levels. Focusing on introducing French culture as well as language, the Institut de Langue Française has a wide range of options ranging from business French (available evenings) to French cooking.

- **Institut Parisien**
  87, blvd de Grenelle; 75015 Paris
  Tel: (01) 4056-0953; email: info@institut-parisien.com;
  Website: http://www.institut-parisien.com
  New courses weekly for students of all levels, with a class size limited to 12. Additional classes include French cuisine, fashion, literature and civilisation.

Entertainment and Leisure

Most cities in France offer a wide range of entertainment possibilities, from major international art and music festivals to local cultural (and culinary) celebrations. Needless to say, if you're in Paris, there will never be a shortage of things to do, whether it be the cinema, the latest exhibition at Beaubourg, the opera or rollerblading along the Seine on a Sunday afternoon. Depending on what you are in the mood for, you will be sure to find it in some form or another—as long as you know where to look!

Cultural Activities

The two Paris weeklies, *Pariscope* (http://www.pariscope.com) and *l'Officiel des Spectacles*, can be bought for a minimal price at any *kiosque* in town. Inside, you will find listings for every movie, theatre and opera performance, museum exhibition and music concert playing for the week, as well as activities for the children. A relatively new weekly, *Zurban* (http://www.zurban.com), includes detailed reviews and articles, in addition to the information listed above. There are English language publications such as *Time Out: Paris* (http://www.timeout.com/paris) and the *Paris Free Voice* (http://www.parisvoice.com) that also list a selection of major events around town.

Outside of Paris, check the weekend sections in the local newspapers for listings of both cultural and sports events. Also, take a trip to the local *mairie* for a list of tourist attractions in the area. And check out the *Syndicate d'Initiative* in each town.

Eating Out

When in France, do as the French do... and take time out to enjoy the local cuisine! *Le Guide Rouge Michelin* (*The Red Guide*; http://www.viamichelin.com) and Gault-Millau (French—http://www.gaultmillau.fr; English—http://www. gayot.com) are probably the two most renowned restaurant guides in France. And they give websites of restaurants so you can make reservations online.

Don't be intimidated into believing that their standards are the only standards. (Your savings account will regret it!) The French are an opinionated bunch, especially when it comes to food. Ask around, see what everybody has to say! Word of mouth and an adventurous spirit continue to be the most successful combination for finding great places to eat.

If all else fails, there is always *Time Out: Paris*'s website (http://www.timeout.com/paris) which also offers some inspiring choices.

Classes, Clubs and Sports

The local *la mairie* (town hall) will have information on classes, clubs, sports facilities and activities in the area in which you live. There is usually a small pamphlet, which you can pick up for free, listing this information. Note that each *arrondissement* in Paris has its own *mairie*.

To find a gym or health club, look under *Clubs de Remise en Forme* in the yellow pages (http://www.pagesjaunes.fr). An extremely popular form of exercise/transportation at the moment is rollerblading. On Sundays in Paris, the *quais* are closed to motor traffic, and the cyclists and rollerbladers take full advantage of the extra space. There is a critical mass ride for rollerbladers once a month.

If football (soccer) is your thing, you're in luck. Look in *L'Equippe*, the daily sporting news, for upcoming matches. In Paris, the home team, Paris-Saint Germain, plays at the Parc des Princes in the 16*eme*.

Shopping
Designer clothes

Many designer brand names such as Chanel, Louis Vuitton, and Yves Saint Laurent were born in Paris and still have headquarters here. While you might not be making too many purchases in the haute couture boutiques, they do make for some great shopping excursions.

The most well-known districts for clothing are:

- **Place des Victoires** (1er): *Haute couture* designer boutiques.
- **St. Germain des Prés** (6eme,7eme): Classy boutiques a step down from the designer stores.
- **Rue de Rivoli** (1er, 4eme): More classy boutiques.
- **Les Halles** (1er): Ubiquitous but familiar chain stores such as Gap or Esprit.

Don't you forget the *Pret a Porter* (ready-to-wear) events every October.

For American food and groceries, try the following:

- **Thanksgiving Grocers** (4eme): 14 rue Charles V. Tel: (01) 4277-6829. Stocks American-style groceries.

- **The Real McCoy** (7eme): 194 rue de Grenelle.
  Tel: (01) 4556-9882. Stocks American-style groceries and cooking utensils.

There are also several high-end department stores to be found in most major cities throughout France, including: Galleries Lafayette, Le Printemps, and La Samaritaine. For more detail on shopping in Paris, visit this website: http://www.paris-touristoffice.com.

Bars and Clubs

For reviews of the scintillating bars and clubs of Paris, check the monthly magazines *Nova* or *Les Inrockuptibles* (both available at *kiosques*), *LYLO* (available at clubs throughout the city) or *Time Out: Paris*. There are also a number of English/Irish pubs to be found around town. Look through *FUSAC* for ads or check out http://www.parispubs.com, an online guide to bars in Paris.

Gay/Lesbian

The French government is one of the most supportive of gay rights in the world. The recent passage of the *Pacte Civil de Solidarité* (commonly referred to as PACS) allowing unmarried couples—both straight and gay—to enjoy the same economic and social privileges as married couples, is among the first of its kind in the world. Paris also hosts the largest Gay Pride Parade in Europe each year.

For information on the gay community in Paris, pick up a copy of one of the following magazines: *Têtu, Lesbia,* or *Gay Pied Hobdo*. **The Centre Gai et Lesbien** (3, rue Keller, 11e; tel: (01) 4357-2147), and the **Maison des Femmes** (163, rue de Charenton, 12e; tel: (01) 4343-4113) serve as meeting places and publishers for various groups in Paris. They are both good spots to meet people and find out more about local organisations and activities.

You might also want to visit le Marais (3e, 4e), the largest gay neighbourhood in Paris. Many bars and clubs are located in this area. For more information in English on nightlife, go to *Time Out: Paris* (http://www.timeout.com/paris).

Religions
Religious Institutions
France is traditionally a Catholic country, although at present less than 12 per cent of the population attends church services regularly. In most major cities, you will also be able to find Protestant, Jewish and Muslim centres of worship.

For the latest information on Christian and Jewish services in English in Paris, grab a copy of *FUSAC*. For information on Muslim services, visit the Grande Mosquée in the Latin Quarter, 2, bis place du puits de l'Ermite, 75005 Paris, or try http://www.mosquee-de-paris.com.

English Language Publications
The following publications can be picked up free of charge throughout Paris at tourist attractions, language schools and the American Church in Paris.
- *FUSAC* (France USA Contacts)—Classified ads of all kinds, from employment to personals.
- *Paris Insider's Guide*—Practical guide for internationals who have recently arrived in Paris.
- *Paris Voice*—A collection of reviews of cultural activities, including books, art, music and theatre.
- *Time Out: Paris*—Lists major events around town. Includes helpful maps and reviews of the city by *arrondissement*.

The following newspapers and magazines can be found at most *kiosques* in major cities throughout France.
- *The Economist*
- *Financial Times*
- *International Herald Tribune*
- *Newsweek*
- *Time*
- *USA Today*
- *The Wall Street Journal Europe*

General Helpful Websites
The internet offers endless information about France. Google away! If you want a start, take a look at the following:

Work and Business

- http://www.ccip.fr
  Website of the Chambre de Commerce et d'Industrie de Paris, the French chamber of commerce. Contains information on starting a business in France.

- http://www.paris-anglo.com
  For practical information on living and working in Paris. Also consists of a message board.

- http://www.euro.ecb.int
  A website of the European Central Bank and the national central banks of the Euro area. Provides information and updates on the euro.

News and Information

- http://www.expatica.com/france
  Catered especially to the English-speaking expatriate living and working in France, the site is updated with local and international daily news articles.
- http://www.pagesjaunes.fr
  French yellow pages, in both French and English.
- http://bonjourparis.com
  All sorts of tourist information on Paris.
- http://www.franglo.com
  French Property Report. Both rentals and places to buy all over France.

Food and Leisure

- http://www.fromages.com
  A website dedicated to traditional French cheese. All you ever wanted to know about this gourmet item. Includes suggestions for wine/cheese combinations.
- http://www.paris.org
  The Paris Pages website has a great selection of links to the monuments and museums of Paris.
- http://www.paris-touristoffice.com
  The official tourist guide to Paris. Provides information on children's activities, shopping, nightlife and more.

FURTHER READING

When the first edition of this book was written, there were very few other titles geared to help you deal with the complex social aspects of life among the French. Now, I am happy to say, there are many. Some are fabulous, but everything you read about the history and the people of this wonderful country will help. Our recommended reading list now includes an extensive collection of books geared specifically for your life as a foreigner in France. Many of these should not be missed.

LIVING AMONG THE FRENCH

An American in Paris: Profile of an Interlude Between Two Wars. Genet. 1940.
- Genet is the one of the pen names of Janet Flanner and this book is a collection of essays and profiles of famous people. Also recommended is *Men and Monuments* originally published by The New Yorker magazine.

Darlinghissima: Letters to a Friend. Janet Flanner. Ed. Natalia Danesi Murray. New York: Harvest/HBJ, 1986.

The Europeans. Luigi Barzini. US: Penguin, 1984.

Europeans. Jane Kramer. US: Penguin, 1990.

France Today. John Ardagh. US: Penguin, 1988.

The French. Theodore Zeldin. New York: Kodansha Globe, 1986.

The Identity of France: History and Environment. Fernand Braudel. Trans. Sian Reynolds. US: Harpercollins, 1990.

French Women Don't Get Fat: The Secret of Eating For Pleasure. Mireille Guiliano. US: Knopf, 2004.

Grape Expeditions in France: Bicycle Tours of the Wine Country. Sally Adamson Taylor. US: Sally Taylor & Friends, 1986.

An Intimate History of Humanity. Theodore Zeldin. New York: Harper Perennial, 1996.
- Zeldin, through the life stories of 25 French women, has written a sort of history of human emotions. A fascinating insight not only into modern French life, but humanity's collective memory as well.

A Little Tour Through France. Henry James.
- This is considered a classic now, and the French haven't changed that much, especially in the countryside. (This book has been reproduced a number of times by various publishers. Check with your favourite bookstore.)

Paris Notes: A newsletter for people who love Paris. Monthly. Manhattan Beach CA.

Paris to the Moon. Adam Gopnik. New York: Random House, 2001.
- This collection of entertaining and thought-provoking essays examines the nuances of French/Anglo cultural differences, touching on everything from puppet shows to the 'parallel paper universe' of French bureaucracy.

The People of Paris. Joseph Amber Barry. US: Doubleday & Co., 1966.

The Rules of the Game in Paris. Nathan Constantin Leites. Translated by Derek Coltman. Chicago: University of Chicago Press, 1969.

A Traveller's History of France. Robert Cole. US: Interlink Publishing: 2001 (6th ed).
- For the visitor not the historian, but a helpful reference.

FOOD AND FILM
Wow, so many books on these topics, who knows where to start or stop!

A Food Lover's Guide to France. Patricia Wells. US: Workman, Publishing Company, 1999 (4th ed).
- Also her *Food Lover's Guide to Paris*, both of them excellent restaurant and food guides, approaching the subject of eating from any number of perspectives.

The French at Table. Rudolph Chelminski. US: William Morrow and Company, Inc., 1985.

French Regional Cooking. Anne Willan. US: Arrow. 1983.

The French Through Their Films. Robin Buss. Unger, 1988.

Paris La Nuit Sexy, 20th edition, 1989. Editions Edicart's SARL, 63 rue de la Prévoyance, 94300 Vincennes. Tel: (01) 4365-7370.
- More than you want to know of the seamy side of French life.

HOW-TO—HELP FOR EXPATRIATES IN FRANCE

At Home in Paris: Your Guide to Living in the French Capital. Ed. Caroline Robert. Junior Service League of Paris, 1993.
- The most exhaustive guide to the details of living in the capital city.

Bloom Where You're Planted. Women of the American Church in Paris.
- Annually produced in October, they have passed their 25th year. Excellent for people just coming to live in Paris.

Buying a Home in France: A Complete Guide. Vivienne Menkes-Ivry. New York: Simon & Schuster, 1993.

Coping with France. Fay Sharman. Blackwell Publishers, 1987.

Cultural Misunderstandings: The French-American Experience. Raymonde Carroll. Trans. Carol Volk. Chicago: University of Chicago Press, 1990. (Original title: *Evidences Invisbles*, France: Editions du Seuil, 1987.)

Customs & Etiquette of France. Danielle Robinson. Bravo Books Ltd. 2005.
- Very compact.

European Customs & Manners. Nancy L. Braganti and Elizabeth Devine. Meadowbrook, Inc., 1992 (rev ed).

France-USA Contacts, a monthly available from the American Church in Paris.

France: What to Know & Expect. Betty Springer. Granville Island/Peanut Butter Publishing, 1989.

French or Foe?: Getting the Most Out of Visiting, Living and Working in France. Polly Platt. Illinois: Distribooks: 2003 (3rd ed).
- A very personal and enthusiastic tour of the French cultural personality by a well-connected American who has lived in Paris for decades and specialises in cross-cultural consulting for businesses.

The French Way: Aspects of Behavior, Attitudes, and Customs of the French. Ross Steele. Illinois: Passport Books, 1995.
- Organised alphabetically by subject from accents to xenophobia, the book offers 85 explanations in about as many pages.

French Ways and Their Meaning. Edith Wharton. Berkshire House, 1997 (reprint).
- Even though written during the World War I by Francophile and novelist Wharton, they are still fresh insights.

AAWE Guide to Education. Paris: Association of American Wives of Europeans (AAWE). (6th edition in 2003.)

Health Care Resources in Paris, published by the Community Health Care Committee of the Women's Institute for Continuing Education at the American College in Paris. 1989. Revised regularly.

How to Europe: The Complete Travelers Handbook. John Bermont. Michigan: Murphy & Broad Publishing, 2003 (4th ed).

Vital Issues: How to Survive Officialdom While Living in France. Published by the Association of American Wives of Europeans (AAWE), latest edition 1999.
- Includes issues such as job hunting, marriage, divorce, retirement, real estate as well as wills and inheritance.

Living, Studying, and Working in France. Saskia Reilly and Lorin David Kalisky. New York: Owl Books, 1999.
- A practical guide to getting situated (taxes, work permits, networking) in France.

Paris Inside-Out. by David Applefield and team at Paris-Anglophone. 1995.
- Visit http://www.paris-anglo.com.

Sixty Million Frenchmen Can't Be Wrong. Jean-Benoît Nadeau and Julie Barrow. US: Sourcesbooks, 2003.
- The best analysis of the French way of life, especially from a political perspective.

The Transplanted Woman: A Study of French-American Marriages in France. Gabrielle Varro. Westport CT: Praeger, 1988.

When in France. Christopher Sinclair-Stevenson. New York: Touchstone Books, 1989.

When in France, Do As The French Do. Ross Steele. New York: McGraw-Hill, 2002.

Working in France: The Ultimate Guide to Job Hunting and Career Success a la Francaise. Carol Pineau & Maureen Kelly. Zephyr, 1992.

A Year in the Merde. Stephen Clarke. US: Bantam, 2004; UK: Black Swan, 2005.

A Year in Provence and *Toujours Provence*. Peter Mayle.
- Mayle teaches you to love the French and laugh while you learn. (There are a number of editions available so check with your favourite bookstore.)

FRENCH HISTORY AND LITERATURE

The Rehearsal or any of the other plays of Jean Anouilh. Other plays of note are *Antigone* and *Becket*.

Candide. Voltaire (François Marie Arouet). 1759.
- A philosophical novel examining life's difficulties and evils at the time of the Enlightenment in France. The time we give to something makes it important, Voltaire said, so it is wise to judge carefully how we use our time. (Check with your bookseller for the latest reprint.)

The Celts. Nora Chadwick. UK: Penguin Books, 1971.

Diderot: The Virtue of a Philosopher. Carol Blum. The Viking Press, 1974.

The Ethics of Ambiguity. Simone de Beauvoir.
- Simone de Beauvoir was a lifelong companion of Jean Paul Sartre, the great 20th century existentialist. The two of them believed that man's life is totally his own responsibility, though he tries to absolve that by creating other forces and causes, such as religion.

Les Grands Auteurs Français du Programme. André Lagarde and Laurent Michard, Les Editions Bordas.
- A summary series of French literature, by century, in French.

The Little Prince. Antoine de Saint-Exupéry,
- Written in the 1930s, thi book found popularity all over the world. Espouses the French concept of the nobility of man which began with Voltaire. (Check with your bookseller for the latest reprint.)

The Marquis de Sade. Geofrey Gorer. Liveright Publishing Corp, 1934.

Les Misérables. Victor Hugo. 1862.
A social novel conveying simple, humanistic ideals. (Check for latest reprint.)

Napoleon III and the Rebuilding of Paris. David H. Pinkney Princeton University Press, 1958.

Richelieu and the French Monarchy. C.V. Wedgewood. Collier Books, 1962.

THE FRENCH LANGUAGE

Thousands of books exist to teach you the language. Among them, you might take a look at the less orthodox ones that will help with the way the French really speak.

Merde! and *Merde Encore!* Genevieve. New York: Fireside, 1998.

Street French (Books 1, 2 & 3). David Burke. US: John Wiley & Sons, 1996.

CULTURE SHOCK IN GENERAL

It is comforting to see that culture shock has become a serious field of study in international business, as well as sociology.

Acts of Identity. R. le Page and A. Tabouret-Keller. Cambridge University Press, 1985.

Cultures in Contact: Studies in Cross-cultural interaction. Ed. Stephen Bochner. Pergamon Press Ltd., 1982.

Culture Shock: Psychological Reactions to Unfamiliar Environments. Adrian Furnham and Stephen Bochner. Methuen & Co. Ltd, 1986.
- Good bibliography on the subject.

The Hidden Dimension, The Silent Language and Beyond Culture, all by Edward T. Hall. Anchor Press, Doubleday, 1977.

Intercultural Training: Don't Leave Home Without It. Robert Kohls SIETAR International, 1984.

International Management, a monthly magazine published by McGraw-Hill House, Maidenhead, SL6 2QL Berkshire, England. Tel: (0628) 23-431.

Language Contact and Bilingualism. Rene Appel & Pieter Muysken. Edward Arnold, 1987.

Leaders Sans Frontiers. Franck Gauthey et al. McGraw-Hill, 1988.

Managing Cultural Differences. Philip R Harris and Robert T Moran. Gulf Publishing Co., Revised 1987.

Training for the Multicultural Manager and Training for the Cross-Cultural Mind. Pierre Casse. SIETAR, 1984.

Venturing Abroad: Europe. Robert T Moran. International Management/McGraw-Hill, 1989.

MAPS

There are several excellent series produced by the National Geographic of France/Institute Géographique National/IGN. Their maps are available all across the country and they have a major retail outlet just off the Champs Elysée in Paris. I find these more 'readable' than the more famous Michelin guides, but *chacun à son goût* (each to his taste). The Relais et Châteaux folks also produce good maps.

If you are driving or cycling in Paris you will need a map showing the one-way (*sens unique*) streets.

ABOUT THE AUTHOR

Sally Adamson Taylor is the product of two distinct American cultures. Her father's family was from New York City and her mother's from Richmond, Virginia. She grew up in between, in Baltimore, Maryland. The American Civil War ended before any of her grandparents were born, but she struggled with it from childhood, and from both sides.

She learned that 'reality' depended on one's cultural perspective. She took readily to journalism and was Managing Editor of the *Boston University News* when she graduated in 1970. (The next year the paper was kicked off campus for being too radical.) A year vagabonding through Europe and North Africa hooked her on the international life.

She settled for a while in San Francisco, working her way 'up' from reporter to editor to publisher. Deciding she liked the first job best, she headed for Hong Kong and became a freelance writer.

Her home base is still a Victorian cottage in San Francisco though she has spent more than two decades travelling the world, with perches in Paris and in Hong Kong. She has written for a wide range of publications, including *The Asian Wall Street Journal* and *The International Herald Tribune*. She wrote the only guide to the wine country of France by bicycle, *Grape Expeditions in France*.

For the last 20 years she has been a foreign correspondent for *Publishers Weekly*, covering the book publishing business in Asia, Africa and the Americas. At the age of 50, she fell in love with sailing and is now off discovering the planet from yet another cultural perspective, the water.

Contributor

Christopher Pitts updated and revised the 2003 edition of this book. During the five years between his first and second trip to France, he was either living in China, or studying Chinese. Nevertheless, he was never able to completely shake the mysterious feeling that France might be his true home. He finally packed up his calligraphy brushes, moved to Paris, and began his first serious study of the seemingly incomprehensible Gallic world. He is now married to a French woman and they are raising their first child in Paris.

INDEX

256

Titles in the CULTURE**SHOCK**! series:

Argentina	Hong Kong	Paris
Australia	Hungary	Philippines
Austria	India	Portugal
Bahrain	Indonesia	San Francisco
Barcelona	Iran	Saudi Arabia
Beijing	Ireland	Scotland
Belgium	Israel	Sri Lanka
Bolivia	Italy	Shanghai
Borneo	Jakarta	Singapore
Brazil	Japan	South Africa
Britain	Korea	Spain
Cambodia	Laos	Sweden
Canada	London	Switzerland
Chicago	Malaysia	Syria
Chile	Mauritius	Taiwan
China	Mexico	Thailand
Costa Rica	Morocco	Tokyo
Cuba	Moscow	Turkey
Czech Republic	Munich	Ukraine
Denmark	Myanmar	United Arab
Ecuador	Nepal	Emirates
Egypt	Netherlands	USA
Finland	New York	Vancouver
France	New Zealand	Venezuela
Germany	Norway	Vietnam
Greece	Pakistan	

For more information about any of these titles, please contact any of our Marshall Cavendish offices around the world (listed on page ii) or visit our website at:

www.marshallcavendish.com/genref